Dear Helen,

You + Dent are a blessing to our church. I pray this book blesses you as you have blessed me!

2014

Rom 1:16

THE GOSPEL
OF
OUR GRANDFATHERS

Preserving the Good News
for
Future Generations

J. A. WHITE

CROSSBOOKS
PUBLISHING

CrossBooks™
A Division of LifeWay
1663 Liberty Drive
Bloomington, IN 47403
www.crossbooks.com
Phone: 1-866-879-0502

First published by CrossBooks 8/05/2013

ISBN: 978-1-4627-3030-8 (sc)
ISBN: 978-1-4627-3029-2 (hc)
ISBN: 978-1-4627-3028-5 (e)

Library of Congress Control Number: 2013913590

Printed in the United States of America.

This book is printed on acid-free paper.

ACKNOWLEDGEMENTS

It would be an exercise in futility to attempt to name and honor every man, deceased and living, who has blessed me by their faithful proclamation of the gospel. There is a host of faithful witnesses in glory that finished their earthly pilgrimage having faithfully and passionately transferred the precious gospel of Jesus Christ by word and pen. By God's grace, there are giants in the land today who are faithfully proclaiming the true, scandalous, powerful, God-glorifying, and man-abasing gospel. I am grateful for each of these men and pray that those living would continue to labor, by the Spirit's power, to prophesy to dead bones that they may live!

(I would like to extend a special note of honor to Dr. Rick Walston of Columbia Evangelical Seminary. Thank you for your encouragement and assistance in the production of this book. May the Lord continue to bless you as much as you have blessed me.)

INTRODUCTION

It is with fear and trembling that I put forth this meager project. My earnest and heartfelt prayer for every soul who endeavors to engage this book is that, by a gracious act of God, they see and embrace Jesus Christ as the risen and exalted Lord of all. Peter boldly and accurately declared, "And there is salvation in no one else, for there is no other name under heaven given among men by which we must be saved" (Acts 4:12). If my labors produce a harvest of but a single soul, I am content. If providence would have the truth contained in this small work fall into the hands of a hungry heart who feasts upon the Bread of Life, I am satisfied as well.

Allow me to give an explanation regarding the title, *The Gospel of Our Grandfathers: Preserving the Good News for Future Generations.* At the publishing of this book, I am the happy father of four children. As I was musing about what kind of spiritual atmosphere they would grow up in (if the Lord delays his coming), I was overwhelmed by the desire to pen a simple work that would bring the reader face-to-face with the attributes of God, the plight of man, the excellence and sufficiency of Christ, the application of redemption, and the assurance of salvation. Though far from exhaustive, it is my aim to "not shrink from declaring to you the whole counsel of God" (Acts 20:27). If I could pass on a singular memoir to my children that vividly displayed the consuming passion of my blood-bought life, the message in the pages to follow would suffice. I pray that you, dear reader, along with my children, would come to embrace and adore Jesus Christ.

What's in the Book?

The psalmist records that God says, "These things you have done, and I have been silent; you thought that I was one like yourself . . ." (Psalm 50:21). In light of such mental idolatry, the first section of *The Gospel of Our Grandfathers* is dedicated to orienting the reader toward a *biblical* view of God. Knowing the God of Scripture will serve to destroy the idols of our minds and hearts that often rob us of the joy of truly worshiping God.

The second section of this book serves as a mirror made of papyrus that enables man to see himself as he truly is before God. In an age in which self-esteem is often valued at a higher premium than biblical truth, the Scripture's verdict regarding the state of man is shocking, scandalous, and absolutely accurate.

The third section of this book is the *magnum opus*. It is here that Christ's life, death, and resurrection take center stage. The glorious, shocking, beautiful, and scandalous truth of the work of Christ on the cross is put forth in an effort to display the majesty and superiority of Jesus Christ.

The fourth section of this book examines the demand of the gospel message: repent and believe. Jesus, at the outset of his earthly ministry, declared, "The time is fulfilled, and the kingdom of God is at hand; repent and believe in the gospel" (Mark 1:15).

Lastly, section five puts forth biblical principles for examining one's life in order to obtain assurance of salvation. A healthy scriptural self-examination is a means of grace that leads to perseverance and should be actively sought: "I write these things to you who believe in the name of the Son of God that you may know that you have eternal life" (1 John 5:13).

Though men of greater esteem and spiritual stature than this author have set themselves to the task of proclaiming and explaining the gospel of Jesus Christ, it is nevertheless my desire to assist the true church (present and future) by contending "for the faith that was once for all delivered to the saints" (Jude 3). Our grandfathers, men of Godly zeal who handled the Scriptures with excellence, integrity, and passion (2 Timothy 2:15), would have us deliver the gospel, in all its full-orbed glory, to future generations because the "gospel is the power of God for salvation to everyone who believes" (Romans 1:16). May the Lord bestow grace upon you as you read *The Gospel of Our Grandfathers*.

TABLE OF CONTENTS

CHAPTER ONE

The God in Need of Nothing (His Self-Existence)

"The God who made the world and everything in it, being Lord of heaven and earth, does not live in temples made by man, nor is he served by human hands, as though he needed anything, since he himself gives to all mankind life and breath and everything" (Acts 17:24-25).

God does not *need* us. These five words deliver a crushing blow to our self-centered tendency to don papier-mâché crowns and declare ourselves the kings and queens of the universe. Of all of the attributes to be examined in the following pages, I felt it was proper to waste no time in knocking the props out from underneath those who think otherwise by pointing to this fact in order that they may see God as he is and worship him accordingly. In his seminal work, *Institutes of the Christian Religion*, John Calvin writes regarding the striking immensity of God:

> My meaning is: we must be persuaded not only that
> as he once formed the world, so he sustains it by his
> boundless power, governs it by his wisdom, preserves it
> by his goodness, in particular, rules the human race with
> justice and judgment, bears with them in mercy, shields
> them by his protection; but also that not a particle of

3

light, or wisdom, or justice, or power, or rectitude, or
genuine truth, will anywhere be found, which does not
flow from him, and of which he is not the cause; in this
way we must learn to expect and ask all things from
him, and thankfully ascribe to him whatever we receive.
. . . For, until men feel that they owe everything to God,
that they are cherished by his paternal care, and that he
is the author of all their blessings, so that naught is to
be looked for away from him, they will never submit to
him in voluntary obedience; no, unless they place their
entire happiness in him, they will never yield up their
whole selves to him in truth and sincerity.[2]

God's self-existence[3] means that he does not need his creation and
is dependent upon no one. Although this may shock the conscience of
many modern churchgoers, it is a well-established biblical fact. The Lord
declares, "For every beast of the forest is mine, the cattle on a thousand
hills. I know all the birds of the hills, and all that moves in the field is
mine. If I were hungry, I would not tell you, for the world and its fullness
are mine" (Psalm 50:10-12). Contrary to popular thought, God did not
create man because he was lonely. Moreover, God did not create man
because he needed his worship, as if man's worship added anything to
God's perfection. God created man solely for his glory. A. W. Pink
states:

---

2   John Calvin, *Institutes of the Christian Religion* (Peabody, MA: Hendrickson
Publishers, Inc., 2008), pp. 7-8.

3   The term self-existence in relation to God does not mean that He caused Himself
to exist, or that He created Himself. It means simply that God does not depend on
anyone or anything for His existence. He is uncaused. God has always existed. On the
other hand, contingent beings (such as humans) depend on someone or something else
for their existence and for their continued existence. Since God is self-existent and is
dependent upon no one and nothing, this also means that God cannot stop existing.
Also referred to as *aseity*.

God was under no constraint, no obligation, no necessity to create. That he chose to do so was purely a sovereign act on his part, caused by nothing outside himself, determined by nothing but his own mere good pleasure . . . That he did create was simply for his *manifestative* glory. . . . God is no gainer even from our worship. He was in no need of that external glory of his grace which arises from his redeemed, for he is glorious enough in himself without that.[4]

The Persons of the Godhead (Trinity) have been fully and completely satisfied in one another since eternity past. Regarding the self-existence of God, Wayne Grudem states that

. . . among the persons of the Trinity there has been perfect love and fellowship and communication for all eternity. The fact that God is three persons yet one God means that there was no loneliness or lack of personal fellowship on God's part before creation. In fact, the love and interpersonal fellowship, and the sharing of glory, have always been and will always be far more perfect than any communion we as finite human beings will ever have with God.[5]

The Psalms also point to the eternal self-existence of God: "Before the mountains were brought forth, or ever you had formed the earth and the world, from everlasting to everlasting you are God" (Psalm 90:2). All of this is necessary in order to force sinful men and women to take their eyes off themselves and gaze upon the glory and immensity of the

---

4   A. W. Pink, *The Attributes of God* (Grand Rapids, MI: Baker Books, 1975), p. 10.

5   Wayne Grudem, *Systematic Theology: An Introduction to Biblical Doctrine* (Grand Rapids, MI: Zondervan, 2000), p. 499.

God of the Bible. In an age of self-absorption, the doctrine of God's self-existence and the reality that he was under no obligation to create man, beast, or planet acts as a proverbial smelling salt to the nostrils of sleeping mortals. It is in the light of this gloriously humbling truth that God's sovereign choice to create man in his image shines the brightest. God, through Isaiah, reveals his gracious heart by declaring, "I will say to the north, Give up, and to south, Do not withhold; bring my sons from afar and my daughters from the end of the earth, everyone who is called by my name, whom I created for my glory, whom I formed and made" (Isaiah 43:6-7). Glorious revelation! Astounding truth! The self-existent God chose to create man from dust for his own glory (see Genesis 2:7). Though perhaps it is not the emotive sentimentality of much modern preaching, the reality that God sovereignly chose to create man for his glory should humble the proudest hearts and cause the most rigid legs to bend. God has chosen to create men and women, and they are accountable to him.

CHAPTER TWO

The God Who Never Changes
(His Immutability)

In a world of shifting sand, the concept of people remaining steadfast in their character and never failing in their promises is difficult to envision. A man's mind is often filled to overflowing with contrary emotions and intentions. Unlike his creation, the God of Scripture is *immutable*[6]. Grudem defines God's immutability as follows: "God is unchanging in his being, perfections, purposes, and promises, yet God does act and feel emotions, and he acts and feels differently in response to different situations."[7] The Scriptures attest that God does not change, that he is like a rock upon which all other lesser forces are smashed. James declares, "Every good gift and every perfect gift is from above, coming down from the Father of lights with whom there is no variation or shadow due to change" (James 1:17). Pink offers the following observation regarding God's unchangeableness:

---

6   It should be noted that some theologians see a contradiction between God's immutability and his prerogative to change his emotions. Though he does *not* have sinful emotions, it is my conviction that the Scriptures clearly teach that he certainly does have and express emotions.

7   Grudem, *Systematic Theology*, p. 163.

Immutability is one of the divine perfections which is not sufficiently pondered. It is one of the excellencies of the Creator which distinguishes him from all his creatures. God is perpetually the same: subject to no change in his being, attributes, or determinations.[8]

What can be said of man's woeful lack of integrity in light of God's honorable veracity? Moses employs his tongue and waxes eloquent when he sings, "The Rock, his work is perfect, for all his ways are justice. A God of faithfulness and without iniquity, just and upright is he" (Deuteronomy 32:4).

The implications of God's immutability are far-reaching indeed. If he were subject to change, morphing from a benevolent creator to a cosmic tyrant, life for mere mortals would be miserable and hopeless. If he were to wantonly renegotiate the terms of his promises and covenants, man would have no rest or peace. As it is, he is a God worthy of trust because he does not roll along with the wind as sea foam. The psalmist exults in God's character by saying, "The counsel of the Lord stands forever, the plans of his heart to all generations" (Psalm 33:11). Elsewhere God himself declares, "I have spoken, and I will bring it to pass; I have purposed, and I will do it" (Isaiah 46:11). In their examination of the works of Puritan theologian Stephen Charnock, Joel Beeke and Mark Jones state the following regarding God's unchangeableness:

> In summary, God's attribute of immutability is too clear and too vital to affirm hesitantly or with reservations. If God's essence is changed then it can only be changed by a being more powerful than God. Such a view was clearly out of the question for Charnock and those who shared his doctrine of God. True, there are passages in Scripture that

---

8   Pink, *The Attributes of God*, p. 46.

"These things you have done, and I have been silent; *you thought that I was one like yourself.* But now I rebuke you and lay the charge before you" (Psalm 50:21, emphasis added).[1]

"Get you up to a high mountain, O Zion, herald of good news; lift up your voice with strength, O Jerusalem, herald of good news; lift it up, fear not; say to the cities of Judah, 'Behold your God!'" (Isaiah 40:9).

1   Unless otherwise indicated, all Scripture is from the *English Standard Version* (Good News Publishers, Copyright © 2001, 2002, 2007).

☩

❧ PART ONE ❧

BEHOLD YOUR GOD –
KNOWING THE GOD
OF SCRIPTURE

seem to imply that God can change His mind, but there are a great deal more texts that affirm God's immutability in regard to His being and knowledge.[9]

It should be the source of a thousand joys for a believer to learn that the God of Scripture is an unchanging, immovable God. He is not a God of shadows, fog, or vain speculation. He is knowable and his Word is unfailing. Jesus, being one with God the Father in essence, is said to be "the same yesterday and today and forever" (Hebrews 13:8). What a clear and poignant affirmation of deity! What a fountain of encouragement to know that "God is light, and in him is no darkness at all" (1 John 1:5). Moreover, the God who reveals himself in Scripture also reveals his steadfastness, which serves as a bulwark to the child of God who walks, lives, and breathes by faith in the Lord. This attribute of God is also a herald of warning to the unsaved. James Montgomery Boice states:

> If it is true that the sovereignty, holiness and omniscience of God are unlikable concepts to the natural man, then it is clear that the fact that God will not change in any of these areas is even more disturbing. The unsaved person would not be so troubled by God's sovereignty if he could think that one day God would become less sovereign and the individual more autonomous. . . . But the immutability of God means that God will always be sovereign, always be holy, always be omniscient.[10]

---

9 Joel R. Beeke and Mark Jones, *A Puritan Theology: Doctrine for Life* (Grand Rapids, MI: Reformation Heritage Books, 2012), p. 66.

10 James Montgomery Boice, *Foundations of the Christian Faith: A Comprehensive and Readable Theology* (Downers Grove, IL: InterVarsity Press, 1986), pp. 143-144.

✝

CHAPTER THREE

The God Who is Everywhere (His Omnipresence)

God's omnipresence, possibly one of the most understated of all his attributes, is worthy of our attention and adoration. Unlike the pantheist who declares that everything is part of an all-encompassing, impersonal deity, the God of Scripture is outside of and superior to his creation yet is intimately involved with it. God is unlimited with respect to space and is present at every point of creation. Grudem defines this attribute as follows: "God does not have size or spatial dimensions and is present at every point of space with his whole being, yet God acts differently in different places."[11] One of the most striking declarations of God's omnipresence appears in the book of Jeremiah:

> Am I a God at hand, declares the Lord, and not a God far away? Can a man hide himself in secret places so that I cannot see him? declares the Lord. Do I not fill heaven and earth? declares the Lord (Jeremiah 23:23-24).

---

11 Grudem, *Systematic Theology*, p. 173.

Our first parents, after committing high treason, illustrated the futility of hiding from God. Scripture states that "the man and his wife hid themselves from the presence of the Lord God among the trees of the garden (Genesis 3:8). How often sinful men repeat their folly only to find that God is relentlessly inescapable. David declares:

Where shall I go from your Spirit? Or where shall I flee from your presence? If I ascend to heaven, you are there! If I make my bed in Sheol, you are there! If I take the wings of the morning and dwell in the uttermost parts of the sea, even there your hand shall lead me, and your right hand shall hold me (Psalm 139:7-10).

For the child of God, this revelation of God's being is staggeringly assuring. If one of his beloved should be swallowed up by the earth, cast into the deepest dungeon, or plunged to the depths of the sea, the shepherd of Psalm 23 is present to comfort. In contrast, David reveals that God is also present in hell to punish. The only proper response to such a realization as this is to bow down in awe and worship the God who is inescapable.

Of God's being, we must realize the vast difference between the creator and the creation. Regarding God's physical proportions, Grudem states the following:

> God is a being who exists *without* size or dimensions in space. In fact, before God created the universe, there was no matter or material so there was no space either. Yet God still existed. Where was God? He was not in a place that we could call a "where," for there was no "where" or space. But God still was! This fact makes us realize that God relates to space in a far different way than we do or than any created thing does. He exists as a kind of being that is far different and far greater than we can imagine.[12]

---

12 Ibid., pp. 174-175.

When we stop to reflect on the implications of God's omnipresence, we are brought face-to-face with our true station: small, finite, limited, and weak. In light of the fact that God is fully present at *every* point of his creation, we can almost hear his ancient exchange with Job ringing in our ears:

> Where were you when I laid the foundation of the earth? Tell me, if you have understanding. Who determined its measurements – surely you know! Or who stretched the line upon it? On what were its bases sunk, or who laid its cornerstone, when the morning stars sang together and all the sons of God shouted for joy? Or who shut in the sea with doors when it burst out from the womb, when I made clouds its garment and thick darkness its swaddling band, and prescribed limits for it and set bars and doors, and said, 'Thus far shall you come, and no farther, and here shall your proud waves be stayed'? Have you commanded the morning since your days began, and caused the dawn to know its place, that it might take hold of the skirts of the earth, and the wicked be shaken out of it? (Job 38:4-13).

God's piercing examination of Job is captured in four consecutive chapters. In the end, Job's response should be the confession of everyone who comes to grips with the enormity of God: "I had heard of you by the hearing of the ear, but now my eye sees you; therefore I despise myself, and repent in dust and ashes" (Job 42:5-6). An inescapable God is a blessing to some and a scourge to others. May we all, like Job, repent and seek his mercy and grace!

CHAPTER FOUR

The God Who is Outside of Time (His Eternality)

As finite beings, we march to the droning of a ticking clock every day of our earthly journey. We live in an uninterrupted succession of seconds until we breathe our last breath and step into eternity. Therefore, the concept of *timelessness* is as foreign to us as hiking in the Rockies is to a salmon. In contrast to our slavish captivity to time, God stands outside of time and is untouched by its effects. Returning to the song of Psalm 90, we see a vivid declaration of God's eternality:

> Before the mountains were brought forth, or ever you had formed the earth and the world, from everlasting to everlasting you are God. You return man to dust and say, "Return, O children of man!" For a thousand years in your sight are but as yesterday when it is past, or as a watch in the night (Psalm 90:2-4).

Jesus, being coeternal with the Father, makes a direct claim to being *the* eternal deity when he exclaimed, ". . . before Abraham was, I am" (John 8:58). The apostle Paul also declares that Jesus is "the image of the invisible God, the firstborn of all creation. For by him all things were created . . . all things were created through him and for him" (Colossians 1:15-16). What a magnificently humbling truth to contemplate! The triune God (Father, Son, and Spirit) has existed from eternity past and will continue to exist for eternity to come. One can only exclaim with David, "What is man that you are mindful of him, and the son of man that you care for him?" (Psalm 8:4). God is the "Alpha and Omega . . . who is and who was and who is to come, the Almighty" (Revelation 1:8). Let us banish all inferior thoughts of him to the heap of idols that our wayward hearts relentlessly produce. Let us join with the Puritan author who gushed:

> O fountain of all good, destroy in me every lofty thought, break pride to pieces and scatter it to the winds, annihilate each clinging shred of self-righteousness, implant in me true lowliness of spirit, abase me to self-loathing and self-abhorrence, open in me a fount of penitential tears, break me, then bind me up; thus will my heart be a prepared dwelling for my God . . . O Holy Trinity, three Persons and one God, inhabit me, a temple consecrated to thy glory. . . . Nothing exceeds thy power, nothing is too great for thee to do, nothing too good for thee to give. Infinite is thy might, boundless thy love, limitless thy grace, glorious thy saving name.[13]

Another lofty consideration regarding God's eternality centers on the fact that he can and does declare future events with pinpoint accuracy. Being outside of time, God alone has the prerogative to know and make known that which will undoubtedly come to pass:

---

13   Arthur Bennett, *The Valley of Vision: A Collection of Puritan Prayers and Devotions* (Carlisle, PA: The Banner of Truth Trust, 2011), pp. 8-9.

Remember this and stand firm, recall it to mind, you
transgressors, remember the former things of old; for
I am God, and there is no other; I am God, and there
is none like me, declaring the end from the beginning
and from ancient times things not yet done, saying,
"My counsel shall stand, and I will accomplish all my
purpose," calling a bird of prey from the east, the man
of my counsel from a far country. I have spoken, and I
will bring it to pass; I have purposed, and I will do it
(Isaiah 46:8-11).

Though it will be dealt with in greater detail later, it is necessary to
highlight God's eternality in relation to his sovereign purposes. In the
book of Revelation, we are afforded a glimpse into God's perspective of
eternity in relation to events that occur in time: "everyone whose name
has not been written *before the foundation of the world* in the book of life
of the Lamb who was slain" (Revelation 13:8, emphasis added). Though
Jesus died on a specific day at a certain time (see Luke 23:44), God saw
this grand, climactic event as a present reality in his consciousness from
all eternity. God is clearly a being that dwells outside of time, unhindered
by its effects. In addition to this, God also acts in time: "Because he
has fixed a day on which he will judge the world in righteousness by a
man whom he has appointed; and of this he has given assurance to all
by raising him from the dead" (Acts 17:31). What an awesome creator!
People need only consider their fragile existence, the incessant passing
of time, and their complete powerlessness in foretelling events to see the
terrible greatness of the God of the Bible. The triune, eternal God rules
over time, acts in time, and yet is completely unbound by its snare.

CHAPTER FIVE

The God Who Knows All Things
(His Omniscience)

If sinful man cannot physically hide from God, he takes refuge in the citadel of his darkened mind. There, in his laboratory of lust, anger, jealousy, or racism, he relishes his wicked thoughts under the false assumption that God is unaware. He may even, if opportunity and temptation collide, act on his hidden intentions, stepping out onto the shaky bridge of ill-fated presumption. It is at this point that David cries out: "You know when I sit down and when I rise up; you discern my thoughts from afar" (Psalm 139:2). The God of the Bible is an all-knowing God; he is omniscient. Writing on God's attributes, John M. Frame makes the following helpful observation:

> Wicked people often think that God will not notice what they do, but they will find that God does know, and that he will certainly condemn their sins. . . . To the righteous, however, God's knowledge is a blessing of the covenant. . . . He knows what is happening to them, he hears their prayer, and he will certainly answer.[14]

---

14   John M. Frame, *The Doctrine of God: A Theology of Lordship Volume 2* (Phillipsburg, NJ: P&R Publishing Company, 2002), p. 484.

Scripture describes him as one who is "perfect in knowledge" (Job 37:16) and whose "understanding is beyond measure" (Psalm 147:5). The God of Scripture is infinitely different from the caricature of much modern preaching in which he is a kindhearted old man who loves it when his children come for tea and conversation. From this view, he is often seen as either ignorant or indifferent to the affairs of man. Nothing could be further from the truth: "And no creature is hidden from his sight, but all are naked and exposed to the eyes of him to whom we must give an account" (Hebrews 4:13).

Peter, the rough-hewn disciple, displays acute spiritual insight when he declares of Jesus, "Lord, you know *everything*" (John 21:17, emphasis added). This is not mere poetry; this is a statement of fact. The very exercise of a finite being attempting to comprehend the implications of God's omniscience is the epitome of futility. The Lord says:

> For my thoughts are not your thoughts, neither are your ways my ways, declares the Lord. For as the heavens are higher than the earth, so are my ways higher than your ways and my thoughts than your thoughts. For as the rain and the snow come down from heaven and do not return there but water the earth, making it bring forth and sprout, giving seed to the sower and bread to the eater, so shall my word be that goes out from my mouth; it shall not return to me empty, but it shall accomplish that which I purpose, and shall succeed in the thing for which I sent it (Isaiah 55:8-9).

In this passage, we see that God's knowledge does not change, evolve, or grow. He knows *all* things, actual and possible. His knowledge is not contingent upon his learning anything, he cannot learn since he already possesses all knowledge. With the eloquence and fervor that has come to be associated with his name, the great Charles Spurgeon offered the following insight regarding God's omniscience:

God Almighty, from his very essence and nature, must be an omniscient God. Strike out the thought that He sees me, and you extinguish Deity by a single stroke. There would be no God if that God had no eyes, for a blind God is no God at all. We could not conceive Him. Stupid as idolaters may be, it is very hard to think that even they had fashioned a blind god. Even they have given eyes to their gods, though they do not see. Juggernaut has eyes stained with blood. Also, the gods of the ancient Romans had eyes, and some of them were called far-seeing gods. Even the heathen can scarcely conceive of a god who had no eyes to see, and certainly we are not so mad as to imagine for a single second that there can be a Deity who lacks the knowledge of everything that is done by man beneath the sun.[15]

What a glorious and terrible truth. The eyes of Almighty God are not the dim eyes of a senile widower who spends his days tending his garden, waiting as it were for his wayward children to grace him with their presence. He is the Lord of glory who knows and sees *all* things. For better or worse, we may all declare with Hagar, "You are a God of seeing" (Genesis 16:13).

---

15 Charles Haddon Spurgeon, "God's Omniscience," in *Classic Sermons on the Attributes of God*, compiled by Warren W. Wiersbe (Grand Rapids, MI: Hendrickson Publishers, Inc., 1989), p. 123.

✝

CHAPTER SIX

The God Who is Trustworthy (His Faithfulness)

The prayer of the Lord Jesus recorded in John 17 contains a small phrase that possesses the power of an atom bomb: "your word is truth" (John 17:17). Jesus does not say that God's word is *a* truth, but rather that it is *the* truth. Christ refers to himself as "the way, and *the truth*, and the life" (John 14:6, emphasis added). In our relativistic world, the idea that one would be so bold, arrogant, and near-sighted as to declare that his particular God is the fountainhead and sole possessor of truth is unthinkable and is often met with disdain. Nonetheless, the Scriptures reveal God Almighty as a God whose word is completely, unfailingly true and who therefore can be trusted when he speaks and acts. This is sometimes referred to as God's *veracity*. We again turn to the song of Moses to find this claim scripturally validated in no uncertain terms: "A God of faithfulness and without iniquity, just and upright is he" (Deuteronomy 32:4). Grudem sheds further light on this glorious attribute of God by defining it as follows: "God's truthfulness [faithfulness] means that he is the true God, and that all his knowledge and words are both true and the final standard of truth."[16]

---

16 Grudem, *Systematic Theology*, p. 195.

In a world of broken promises, abounding conspiracy theories, flagrant lies, and violated covenants, what a joyous revelation it is to see the God of the Bible revealed as a faithful, trustworthy creator. Scripture abundantly attests to this divine truth. "And this is eternal life, that they know you the only true God, and Jesus Christ whom you have sent" (John 17:3). "But the Lord is the true God; he is the living God and the everlasting King" (Jeremiah 10:10). "Every word of God proves true; he is a shield to those who take refuge in him" (Proverbs 30:5). "Lying lips are an abomination to the Lord, but those who act faithfully are his delight" (Proverbs 12:22).

In the Hebrew tongue, he is called *Jehovah El-Emeth* (the Lord God of Truth). In light of this, the psalmist declares, "Your decrees are very trustworthy; holiness befits your house, O Lord, forevermore" (Psalm 93:5). In another place he exults, "The works of his hands are faithful and just; all his precepts are trustworthy" (Psalm 111:7). Jesus reveals that one of the evils that pour forth from a man's fallen nature is "deceit" (Mark 7:22). The Lord declares that liars will be among the eternally damned (Revelation 21:8). What a chasm of difference exists between the blindingly pure words of the faithful God of the Bible and the vile, shifting, and fickle declarations of the creature! His faithfulness (truthfulness) is a wellspring of blessing to his sheep for they know that his promises and grace toward them are sure. When the Son of God beckons, "Come to me, all who labor and are heavy laden, and I will give you rest" (Matthew 11:28), they need not hesitate in heeding his gracious invitation for fear of a renegotiation. For the rebels, however, his faithfulness is stiflingly heavy. For when he decrees, "Not everyone who says to me, 'Lord, Lord,' will enter the kingdom of heaven . . . I will declare to them, 'I never knew you; depart from me, you workers of lawlessness'" (Matthew 7:21, 23), the unsaved must shudder, as they know that the Lord's word is faithful and true. May we all say with the poet:

Thy word is full of promises, flowers of sweet fragrance, fruit of refreshing flavour when culled by faith. May I be made rich in its riches, be strong in its power, be happy in its joy, abide in its sweetness, feast on its preciousness, draw vigour from its manna. Lord, increase my faith.[17]

---

17 Bennett, *The Valley of Vision*, p. 197.

CHAPTER SEVEN

The God Who Gives of Himself (His Love)

"God is love" (1 John 4:8). John, the great apostle, makes a simple yet profound declaration. Many Christians have often misused and misquoted this passage and have, knowingly or unknowingly, created an idol. One may ask, "How can this statement be presented any other way than the plainest meaning?" At this point we must stand fast in the truth that God is perfect in *all* of his attributes. His love is just and his justice is loving and so forth. God cannot and will not negate his holy justice for the sake of expressing his holy love; he is perfect. God's love, since he *is* love, can be defined as his benevolent giving of himself.[18] Nowhere in history do we see God's love manifested in more brilliant radiance than on the cross: "In this is love, not that we have loved God but that he loved us and sent his Son to be the propitiation for our sins" (1 John 4:10). Though we will deal with this topic in much more detail later, it is imperative to point the reader to this passage in order to eradicate false, sentimental, and imperfect ideas of what love is.

The self-giving of God (his love) is inseparably linked to the rugged cross of Calvary. "For God so loved the world, that he gave his only Son, that whoever believes in him should not perish but have eternal life"

---

18 Grudem, *Systematic Theology*, p. 199.

(John 3:16). The apostle Paul utters one of the most strikingly complex statements in the whole of Scripture: "But God shows his love for us in that while we were still sinners, Christ died for us" (Romans 5:8). Sufficed to say, the love of God is seen most clearly in the sacrifice of Jesus Christ. We turn again to the Puritans to glean spiritual insight into the love of God:

> Thou hast been mindful of me and visited me, taken charge of me from birth, cared in all conditions for me, fed me at thy table, drawn the curtains of love around me, given me new mercies every morning. . . . May thy goodness always lead me to repentance, and thy longsuffering prove my salvation.[19]

Yes indeed, may the fact that the Lord of all creation would condescend and give of himself to vile, sinful creatures lead us to broken penitence every day! Obtaining and relishing a scripturally correct view of God's love is as important for us today as it was in the days of A. W. Pink:

> There are many today who talk about the love of God, who are total strangers to the God of love. The Divine love is commonly regarded as a species of amiable weakness, a sort of good-natured indulgence; it is reduced to a mere sickly sentiment, patterned after human emotion. Now the truth is that on this, as on everything else, our thoughts need to be formed and regulated by what is revealed thereon in Holy Scripture. That there is urgent need for this is apparent not only from the ignorance which so generally prevails, but also the low state of spirituality which is now so sadly evident everywhere among professing Christians. How little real love there

---

19   Bennett, *The Valley of Vision*, pp. 210-211.

is for God. One chief reason for this is because our hearts are so little occupied with his wondrous love for his people. The better we are acquainted with his love – its character, fullness, blessedness – the more will our hearts be drawn out in love to him.[20]

Moreover, God's love displayed on the cross empowers his people to love one another: "Beloved, if God so loved us, we also ought to love one another" (1 John 4:11). To reduce God's love down to a flash of (human) emotion or sentimentality is to rob God of his splendor and glory. To attempt to explain the love of God devoid of the sacrifice of Christ, which is the epitome of God's self-giving, is to commit a great atrocity. As we will see in regards to his holiness, God's love is utterly unlike the love of his creatures. Though our love may be fickle and brief, the love of God is sovereign and resolute. The Israelites were not loved by God for any other reason than that "the Lord set his love on you and chose you" (Deuteronomy 7:7). What a bastion of security for the servant of Jesus Christ. That God's love is a sovereign love which is not contingent upon our merit should move us to drink deep from the waters of his character.

---

20 Pink, *The Attributes of God*, p. 99.

CHAPTER EIGHT

The God Who is Good to the Distressed (His Mercy)

"As a father shows compassion to his children, so the Lord shows compassion to those who fear him" (Psalm 103:13). After sinning against the Lord by taking an unauthorized census, David learns of the potential consequences for his sin. David, a man who was not ignorant to the scriptural reality of God's character, cries out, "I am in great distress. Let us fall into the hand of the Lord, for his mercy is great; but let me not fall into the hand of man" (2 Samuel 24:14). David was in great distress and thirsted for God's mercy! One of the most exquisite exaltations of God's mercy appears in the book of Exodus: "The Lord, the Lord, a God merciful and gracious, slow to anger, and abounding in steadfast love and faithfulness" (Exodus 34:6). Let us now be careful to tread wisely across the plain of God's mercy, for his mercy is not inclined to us out of necessity. If being in distress on the part of the creature demanded and controlled the dispersion of mercy on the part of the creator, then all men would receive mercy from the Lord. Being that "all have sinned and fall short of the glory of God" (Romans 3:23), it could be said that every human being is in the *utmost* distress. Pink says that it is "pure sovereign grace which alone determines the exercise of Divine mercy."[21] In light of Paul's affirmation of this fact, little can be refuted: "So then he has mercy on whomever he wills, and he hardens whomever he wills" (Romans 9:18). Though God bestows unmerited mercy upon unregenerate men (see Matthew 5:45), they should not think that their self-imposed distress (sin) can or will solicit merciful treatment from the Almighty.

Having established this fact, let us turn our happy attention to God's mercy toward his people. The apostle Paul offers the following benediction in which we see the relationship between God's mercy toward his children and their free bestowal of mercy toward others:

> Blessed be the God and Father of our Lord Jesus Christ, the Father of mercies and the God of all comfort, who comforts us in all our affliction, so that we may be able to comfort those who are in any affliction, with the comfort with which we ourselves are comforted by God (2 Corinthians 1:3-4).

It is because of the presence of the Good Shepherd among his people that they declare, "Surely goodness and mercy shall follow me all the days of my life, and I shall dwell in the house of the Lord forever" (Psalm 23:6). When his beloved are afflicted, they can cry as the psalmist:

> Behold, as the eyes of servants look to the hand of their master, as the eyes of a maidservant to the hand of her mistress, so our eyes look to the Lord our God, till he has mercy upon us. Have mercy upon us, O Lord, have mercy upon us, for we have had more than enough of contempt. Our soul has had more than enough of the scorn of those who are at ease, of the contempt of the proud (Psalm 123:2-4).

---

21   Pink, *The Attributes of God*, p. 93.

In times of great upheaval, his people may expectantly await the arrival of his mercy, his goodness toward them in their hour of need. A man of greater spiritual stature than this author said it well many years ago:

> Let me tell you that the mercy of God flows freely. It wants no money and no price from you, no fitness of frames and feelings, no preparation of good works or penitence. Free as the brook, which leaps from the mountainside, at which every weary traveler may drink, so free is the mercy of God. Free, as the sun that shines, gilds the mountain's brow, and makes glad the valleys without fee or reward, so free is the mercy of God to every needy sinner. Free, as the air, which belts the earth and penetrates the peasant's cottage as well as the royal palace without purchase or premium, so free is the mercy of God in Christ.[22]

God expresses his goodness to those in distress. To the convicted sinner, this is a hymn that enters the ear as warm medicinal oil. To the child of God, this is likewise a source of great encouragement, as this life is rife with pitfalls and sloughs of despair. God's mercy stands as a lighthouse on the crags amidst the tempest.

---

22 Charles Haddon Spurgeon, "The Mercy of God," in *Spurgeon Gold*, compiled by Ray Comfort (Alachua, FL: Bridge-Logos, 2005), p. 30.

✝

CHAPTER NINE

The God Who Shows Favor to the Unfavorable (His Grace)

In an age of unbridled self-entitlement, the notion of being *unfavorable* is foreign at best and repulsive at worst. Every Lord's Day, little brick buildings throughout the land ring with the sound of melodies that often tell of God's grace. The grace of God is often the *magnum opus* of our hymnody, prose, and preaching. Although it is proper and biblical to joyously exult in the grace of God, the definition of the term is often missed or overlooked. J. I. Packer summarizes God's grace as,

> . . . love freely shown toward guilty sinners, contrary to their merit and indeed in defiance of their demerit. It is God showing goodness to persons who deserve only severity and had no reason to expect anything but severity.[23]

---

23 J. I. Packer, *Knowing God* (Downers Grove, IL: InterVarsity Press, 1973), p. 132.

Though we will examine the grace of God in further detail in a later chapter, we must cast our eyes to Golgotha[24] in order understand and relish God's favor toward sinners.

"For all have sinned and fall short of the glory of God, and are justified by his grace as a gift, through the redemption that is in Christ Jesus" (Romans 3:23-24). Near the end of his three-chapter indictment against sinful humanity in the book of *Romans*, the apostle Paul shines a spotlight on the condition of man and the gracious heart of God. In two successive verses, Paul notes the unfavorable condition of man as that of a rebel against a holy creator and the sovereign benevolence of that creator that flows through the sacrifice of his Son. Elsewhere the great apostle puts forth a stunningly clear and succinct exposition of the salvation bestowed upon guilty men: "For by *grace* you have been saved through faith. And this is not your own doing; it is the *gift* of God, not a result of works, so that no one may boast" (Ephesians 2:8-9, emphasis added). Commenting on God's favor toward the unfavorable, Boice writes:

> For in Jesus we who are sinners can be made righteous. We who are "dead through the trespasses and sins" can be made alive spiritually. The blessings of salvation come, not by fighting against God's ways or by hating him for what we consider to be an injustice, but rather by accepting his verdict upon our true nature as fallen beings and turning to Christ in faith for salvation.[25]

Boice raises a shaky finger and points with trepidation and reverence toward the hill where Christ bore the penalty of his people (see Isaiah 53:4-5). This indeed is where we behold the manifest grace of God:

But the law is not of faith, rather "The one who does them

---

24 The hill on which Christ was crucified

25 Boice, *Foundations of the Christian Faith*, p. 207.

shall live by them." Christ redeemed us from the curse of the law by becoming a curse for us – for it is written, "Cursed is everyone who is hanged on a tree" – so that in Christ Jesus the blessing of Abraham might come to the Gentiles, so that we might receive the promised Spirit through faith (Galatians 3:12-14).

God is perfect in *all* of his attributes. His grace, therefore, is not manifested at the price of a reduction in another attribute. He is completely perfect in every regard (see Matthew 5:48). This point cannot be labored too fervently in light of the tendency of many evangelists, preachers, and those who profess Christ to exalt the grace of God toward sinful, law-breaking men at the expense of God's other attributes. How, for instance, can a holy God show favor to unholy men without himself becoming unholy or imperfect in his character? How can a righteous judge show grace to condemned criminals (see Proverbs 17:15)? When we talk, sing, or preach about the grace of God, we are bound by Scripture and the witness of the Holy Spirit to beat our breasts as the tax collector of Luke 18:13 and embrace the cross of Christ as the sole means of the favor that we enjoy. To this end, Pink states:

> Now the grace of God is manifested in and by and through the Lord Jesus Christ.... This does not mean that God never exercised grace toward any before his Son became incarnate – Genesis 6:8, Exodus 33:19, etc., clearly show otherwise. But grace and truth were fully revealed and perfectly exemplified when the Redeemer came to this earth, and died for his people upon the cross.[26]

---

26 Pink, *The Attributes of God*, pp. 88-89.

CHAPTER TEN

The God Unlike Anything (His Holiness)

I t is here at the contemplation of God's holiness that we draw near to the very throne room of heaven. If you incline your ear, the sounds of eternal praise echo forth from the living creatures stationed in his presence: "Holy, holy, holy is the Lord God Almighty, who was and is and is to come!" (Revelation 4:8). These creatures that are "full of eyes in front and behind" never tire of bellowing forth their one-word chorus as their vision is assaulted by the blinding holiness of God. Interestingly, of all the attributes of God, this one receives thrice the recognition. Jerry Bridges, writing on the threefold declaration of "Holy" found in Isaiah 6, notes: "The Hebrew language uses repetition to indicate emphasis as we do by italics or boldface type. . . . Such a threefold repetition in Hebrew indicates the highest possible degree, or as we could say, the infiniteness of God's holiness."[27] The contemplation of God's holiness should cause the greatest minds among mortal men to wail in sackcloth and ash at their utter inability to grasp the smallest measure of it. The psalmist, meditating on this very thing, cries forth:

---

27 Jerry Bridges, *The Transforming Power of the Gospel* (Colorado Springs, CO: Navpress, 2012), p. 19.

The Lord reigns; let the peoples tremble! He sits enthroned upon the cherubim; let the earth quake! The Lord is great in Zion; he is exalted over all the peoples. Let them praise your great and awesome name! Holy is he! The King in his might loves justice. You have established equity; you have executed justice and righteousness in Jacob. Exalt the Lord our God; worship at his footstool! Holy is he! (Psalm 99:1-5).

Grudem defines God's holiness in the following way: "God's holiness means that he is separated from sin and devoted to seeking his own honor."[28] Is it any wonder that mere creatures, regardless of their stately and magnificent form, cry "Holy" in his presence? A perfectly sinless being is gloriously foreign to the minds of sinful men. Moses sang of what he knew and beheld: "Who is like you, O Lord, among the gods? Who is like you, majestic in holiness, awesome in glorious deeds, doing wonders?" (Exodus 15:11). David declared that the very name of the Lord is holy: "Bless the Lord, O my soul, and all that is within me, bless his holy name!" (Psalm 103:1). Even the demons knew and feared the incarnate God: "What have you to do with us, Jesus of Nazareth? Have you come to destroy us? I know who you are – the Holy One of God" (Mark 1:24). Should we not join with them and exalt the God of Scripture simply on the basis of who he is? In light of such blinding perfection, should we not worship and adore him regardless of his dispersion of blessings? We have much to learn from creatures, who themselves are stunningly brilliant in their design and station, who give themselves to the eternal task of declaring how great is his holiness!

In addition to being separated from sin and devoted to his own honor, God's holiness showcases another striking reality: there is *nothing* like him. Isaiah's prophecy contains a beautiful presentation of the nature and character of God (Isaiah 40:9-31). It is here that a question is asked:

---

28   Grudem, *Systematic Theology*, p. 202.

"To whom then will you liken God, or what likeness compare with him?" (Isaiah 40:18). The deafening response of every intelligent creature should be: "There is none like you among the gods, O Lord, nor are there any works like yours" (Psalm 86:8). Were you to be endowed with the gift of flight, you could search the world over and never find a morsel or mountain that is like God. He is utterly unlike his creation. Any notion of diminishing God's glory in making him to be anything other than the "One who is high and lifted up" (Isaiah 57:15) is blasphemous idolatry.

The God of Scripture is not the *man upstairs*. He is not a cosmic genie whose greatest joy and purpose is to bless man by indulging his every felt need. He is not a white-bearded grandpa who winks at sin and appreciates whatever acknowledgment his creatures remember to give him. He is not laughing along with our improper jokes and sarcastic wit. He is *holy*.

CHAPTER ELEVEN

A God Who is Unified (His Tri-Unity)

The task of accurately and reverently mining the gold of understanding from the doctrine of the Trinity is fraught with theological peril. Great minds of generations past have been humbled by the pondering of such a lofty theme. Heresies abound in regards to the Trinity. *Modalism* (God is a single being that manifests in separate modes), *Arianism* (Jesus was created by the Father), and *subordinationsim* (Jesus was not equal to the father in attributes) are but a few of the ideologies that have assailed the church since its birth. A. W. Tozer captures the inherent tension of this topic in poetic fashion:

> To meditate on the three Persons of the Godhead is to walk in thought through the garden eastward in Eden and to tread on holy ground. Our sincerest effort to grasp the incomprehensible mystery of the Trinity must remain forever futile, and only by the deepest reverence can it be saved from actual presumption. Some persons who reject all they cannot explain have denied that God is a Trinity. Subjecting the Most High to their cold, level-eyed scrutiny, they conclude that it is impossible that He could be both One and Three. These forget that their whole life

is shrouded in mystery. They fail to consider that any real explanation of even the simplest phenomenon in nature lies hidden in obscurity and can no more be explained than can the mystery of the Godhead.[29]

With this recognition we turn our attention to the Scriptures in our mining efforts. In Genesis chapter one, the Lord refers to himself in the plural: "And then God said, 'Let *us* make man in *our* image, after *our* likeness'" (Genesis 1:26, emphasis added). The same plural pronoun is found elsewhere: "Then the Lord God said, 'Behold, the man has become like one of *us* in knowing good and evil'" (Genesis 3:22, emphasis added). In Isaiah's vision of the heavenly throne room, the Lord again states, "... 'Whom shall I send, and who will go for *us*?' Then I said, 'Here am I! Send me'" (Isaiah 6:8, emphasis added). Regarding the need and sufficiency of scriptural revelation of the doctrine of the Trinity, Berkhof states:

> The doctrine of the Trinity is very decidedly a doctrine of revelation. It is true that human reason may suggest some thoughts to substantiate the doctrine, and that men have sometimes on purely philosophical grounds abandoned the idea of a bare unity in God, and introduced the idea of living movement and self-distinction. And it is also true that Christian experience would seem to demand some such construction of the doctrine of God. At the same time it is a doctrine which we would not have known, nor have been able to maintain with any degree of confidence, on the basis of experience alone, and which is brought to our knowledge only by God's special self-revelation.[30]

---

29 A. W. Tozer, *The Knowledge of the Holy* (New York, NY: HarperCollins Publishers, 1961), pp. 27-28).

30 L. Berkhof, *Systematic Theology* (Grand Rapids, MI: WM. B. Eerdman's Publishing Co., 1949), p. 85.

God's self-revelation of his triune nature is heralded throughout the testimony of Scripture. Like the passages previously mentioned, the psalmist also highlights the plural unity of God:

> Your throne, O God, is forever and ever. The scepter of your kingdom is a scepter of uprightness; you have loved righteousness and hated wickedness. Therefore God, your God, has anointed you with the oil of gladness beyond your companions (Psalm 45:6-7).

In this passage, two Persons are referred to as "God." Such a title cannot be bestowed upon even the mightiest and noblest of earthly kings. The writer of the book of *Hebrews* declares, "And again, when he brings the firstborn into the world, he says 'Let all God's angels worship him'" (Hebrews 1:6). Jesus is to be worshiped because he is the second Person of the Trinity. Here again the Scriptures present the reader with a plural view of God's nature. The Father, Son, and Holy Spirit dwell in eternal, perfect unity. The Trinity is summarized in three short statements that are established by the witness of Scripture:

> God is three persons.
> Each person is fully God.
> There is one God.[31]

Any deviation from this simple formula is to tread into heresy. Much about this precious doctrine could be examined and lauded, but the relationship of the Persons of the Trinity will be examined from John's gospel: "In the beginning was the Word, and the Word was with God, and the Word was God" (John 1:1). In order to embrace the satisfying beauty of the cross of Christ, we must cast our eyes on this passage and imagine the beautiful, sinless, and perfectly loving relationship that

---

31   Grudem, *Systematic Theology*, p. 231.

existed between the members of the Trinity. Each was honoring and treasuring one another with perfect love for all eternity. With the sweet aroma of this scene fresh in our nostrils, we must now turn to the cross and hear the son cry, "My God, my God, why have you forsaken me?" (Mark 15:34). The finite human mind and the frail human heart cannot fathom the smallest portion of this declaration from the lips of the "Lamb of God, who takes away the sin of the world!" (John 1:29). I submit to you, dear reader, that the doctrine of the Trinity must be honored if the cross is to be sweet in our estimation. It is here that I turn to the eloquent tongue of a Puritan brother to close our brief and woefully insufficient examination of the Trinity:

> Heavenly Father, blessed Son, eternal Spirit, I adore thee as one Being, one Essence, one God in three distinct Persons, for bringing sinners to thy knowledge and to thy kingdom. O Father, thou hast loved me and sent Jesus to redeem me; O Jesus, thou hast loved me and assumed my nature, shed thine own blood to wash away my sins, wrought righteousness to cover my unworthiness; O Holy Spirit, thou hast loved me and entered my heart, implanted there eternal life, revealed to me the glories of Jesus. Three Persons and one God, I bless and praise thee, for love so unmerited, so unspeakable, so wondrous, so mighty to save the lost and raise them to glory. . . . Let me live and pray as one baptized into the threefold Name.[32]

---

32 Bennett, *The Valley of Vision*, pp. 2-3.

Chapter Twelve

The God Who Does What is Right (His Justice)

Victims of crime and violence cry out for justice and vindication with the expectation that justice will be delivered speedily and objectively. When maladies and catastrophes light upon the sons of men, they often raise a clinched fist to heaven and chastise God for being unjust. Their indictment against the Lord reveals their wicked hearts and darkened understanding, for they betray an ill-fated sense of divine justice. God's justice (righteousness) is intimately related to his sovereignty. Due to the fact that God is the highest and greatest being, he *is* the standard of right by which all lesser matters are gauged. On the subject of God's righteous character, Berkhof writes:

> Justice manifests itself especially in giving every man his due, in treating him according to his deserts. The inherent righteousness of God is naturally basic to the righteousness which He reveals in dealing with his creatures, but is especially the latter, also called the justice of God, that calls for special consideration here. The Hebrew terms for "righteous" and "righteousness" are *tsaddik, tsedhek,* and *tsedhakah,* and the corresponding

Greek terms, *dikaios* and *dikaiosune*, all of which contain the idea of conformity to a standard. This perfection is repeatedly ascribed to God in Scripture.[33]

The psalmist declares, "Righteous are you, O Lord, and right are your rules. . . . Your righteousness is righteous forever, and your law is true" (Psalm 119:137, 142). The resounding witness of the first three chapters of the book *Romans* should cause all demands of justice and recompense to cease on the part of sinful men. Paul points his finger at the whole of humanity as violators of God's law and says:

> What then? Are we Jews any better off? No, not at all. For we have already charged that all, both Jews and Greeks, are under sin, as it is written: "None is righteous, no, not one; no one understands; no one seeks for God. All have turned aside; together they have become worthless; no one does good, not even one" (Romans 3:9-12).

When sinful men cry out for divine justice, they are unknowingly requesting their own demise. In light of Paul's summation of the condition of humanity (transgressors of God's perfect law), divine justice is inclined to deliver pulverizing judgment against it. If God did not punish sin, he would cease to be just. Since his attributes are perfect, if he ceased to be perfect in any one of them, he would cease to be God. The vindication of God's character is the very reason that Paul continues:

> For all have sinned and fall short of the glory of God, and are justified by his grace as a gift, through the redemption that is in Christ Jesus, whom God put forward as a propitiation by his blood, to be received by faith. This was to show God's righteousness, because in his divine

---

33 Berkhof, *Systematic Theology*, p. 75.

forbearance he had passed over former sins. It was to show his righteousness at the present time, so that he might be just and the justifier of the one who has faith in Jesus (Romans 3:23-26).

One may ask, "How could a holy God call an adulterous murder like David a man after his own heart?" Another may join in the fray and cry out, "How could he be a friend to a liar like Abraham?" As Paul declared in the previous passage, the cross stands as a shining beacon to the world that heralds the fact that God's perfect righteousness is intact. Man's sin must be punished. Either a man must suffer for his transgressions, or a perfect substitute must be presented. It is at this juncture that we again turn to Paul:

> For while we were still weak, at the right time Christ died for the ungodly. For one will scarcely die for a righteous person – though perhaps for a good person one would dare even to die – but God shows his love for us in that while we were still sinners, Christ died for us. Since, therefore, we have now been justified [declared to be righteous] by his blood, much more shall we be saved by him from the wrath of God. For if while we were enemies we were reconciled to God by the death of his Son, much more, now that we are reconciled, shall we be saved by his life (Romans 5:6-10).

In the cross of Christ, God's name was vindicated before humanity, angels, and demons. His divine justice that deals with every man according to what he deserves was satisfied on the sinless, wrath-bearing sacrifice of Jesus. God alone, due to his perfection and position as the sovereign ruler of all things, is able to define what is right and what ought to be done. Our vain notions of justice are perverted and fickle, changing with the tide of our emotions and sense of self-preservation. In stark contrast to his creation, God stands alone as the sole judge who is able and willing to dispense divine justice. For those who trust in his gracious offer of reconciliation through the substitutionary death of his son, they find him to be both "just and the justifier of the one who has faith in Jesus" (Romans 3:26). For those who reject the mercy and grace of God, the witness of Scripture rings forth with chilling clarity: "Beloved, never avenge yourselves, but leave it to the wrath of God, for it is written, 'Vengeance is mine, I will repay, says the Lord'" (Romans 12:19). Though carnal men will gnash their teeth in defiance at such a statement, Moses reminds them: "The Rock, his work is perfect, for all his ways are justice. A God of faithfulness and without iniquity, just and upright is he" (Deuteronomy 32:4).

✝

CHAPTER THIRTEEN

The God Who is Unlimited (His Omnipotence)

"Is anything too hard for the Lord?" (Genesis 18:14). In light of God's omnipotence the answer is a thunderous, "No!" If the attribute of omnipotence were granted to any lesser being, every creature in the known universe would be filled with anxious trepidation. Will the king show mercy? Will he utterly destroy us merely for sport? Will he renegotiate his terms of peace with us and scatter us to the wind? These are but a smattering of the justifiable inquiries that would rightly come forth from creation. If a created, finite, imperfect being had absolute power, the results would likely be nauseatingly macabre. It is here that we must (biblically) define our term: "God's omnipotence means that God is able to do all his holy will."[34] At the realization of this insight, all creation breathes a sigh of relief. God alone is sovereign (unbound and externally unconstrained) and omnipotent (all-powerful). He answers to no one and yet he will not deny his own character. Unlike a human despot, the God of Scripture rules and reigns in absolute perfection, free to make his own decrees, and completely able to bring to pass whatsoever he desires.

---

34 Grudem, *Systematic Theology*, p. 216.

In light of this reality, God will not deny himself. Grudem says, "God cannot lie [Titus 1:2], sin [Leviticus 11:44], deny himself [2 Timothy 2:13], or be tempted with evil [James 1:13]. He cannot cease to exist, or cease to be God, or act in a way inconsistent with any of his attributes."[35] It is because of the security found in understanding God's character that Jeremiah could exclaim, "Ah, Lord God! It is you who have made the heavens and the earth by your great power and your outstretched arm! Nothing is too hard for you" (Jeremiah 32:17). We should also exult in the fact that the God of the Bible is not too weak to fulfill his promises. He is not subject to the rule of another authority. He is pure and perfect and therefore will not exercise his power merely to satisfy a lust for dominance or wanton violence. We can joyously echo the angelic response: "For nothing will be impossible with God" (Luke 1:37).

The seed of rebellion that germinates in the hearts of all men sprouts strong roots and thorny shoots when the sunlight of God's sovereign omnipotence shines upon it. Our desire for autonomy often manifests itself at the hearing of a divine declaration such as this:

> What shall we say then? Is there injustice on God's part? By no means! For he says to Moses, "I will have mercy on whom I have mercy, and I will have compassion on whom I have compassion." So then it depends not on human will or exertion, but on God, who has mercy. For the Scripture says to Pharaoh, "For this very purpose I have raised you up, that I might show my power in you, and that my name might be proclaimed in all the earth." So then he has mercy on whomever he wills, and he hardens whomever he wills. You will say to me then, "Why does he still find fault? For who can resist his will?" But who are you, O man, to answer back to God? Will what is molded say to its molder, "Why have you made me like

---

35 Ibid., p. 217.

this?" Has the potter no right over the clay, to make out of the same lump one vessel for honorable use and another for dishonorable use? (Romans 9:14-21).

When sinful men are confronted by the truth of God's perfect sovereignty, they often adjust their papier-mâché crown and settle firmly into their throne of clay. We must see God's omnipotence in light of his utter perfection. We must embrace the totality of Scripture that tells us that "everyone who calls upon the name of the Lord will be saved" (Romans 10:13) and that God sovereignly "chose us in him before the foundation of the world" (Ephesians 1:4). What glorious tension exists in these two truths that force us to our knees in awe of the Lord! To this end, Pink states:

> The sovereignty of God may be defined as the exercise of his supremacy . . . Being infinitely elevated above the highest creature, He is the Most High, Lord of heaven and earth. Subject to none, influenced by none, absolutely independent; God does as he pleases, only as he pleases, always as he pleases. None can thwart him, none can hinder him.[36]

In light of his perfection, we can rest upon the one who "works all things according to the counsel of his will" (Ephesians 1:11). We can trust the God who is able to do "far more abundantly than all that we ask or think" (Ephesians 3:20). We can lay a firm hold upon the promises put forth by the God who says, "So shall my word be that goes out from my mouth; it shall not return to me empty, but it shall accomplish that which I purpose, and shall succeed in the thing for which I sent it" (Isaiah 55:11).

---

36 Pink, *The Attributes of God*, p. 40.

CHAPTER FOURTEEN

The God Devoted to His Own Honor (His Jealousy)

Rest assured dear reader, that if you winced at the reading of the title of this chapter, you are not alone. The word *jealousy* evokes ideas about emotions that are common to the sons of men. The so-called green-eyed monster readily springs to mind. Sinful lusting after power, possessions, or beauty also accompanies the term. What are we to surmise about God being described as jealous? Why are we called to applaud his devotion to his own honor in light of the fact that if any human were to do so it would be denounced as sickening pride? For us fallen humans, *jealousy* is a selfish feeling of resentment against someone because of that person's success or advantages. This is not so for the perfect Deity. There is no one more successful than God. There is no one with advantages that God does not have. God does not have petty jealousy as we humans do. To begin to understand what it means for God to be jealous, we must catch a glimpse of the very nature of God. In his book *Knowing God*, J. I. Packer points directly to the witness of Scripture to establish the basis of God's jealousy:

Were we imagining a God, then naturally we should ascribe to him only characteristics which we admired, and jealousy would not enter the picture. Nobody would *imagine* a jealous God. But we are not making up an idea of God by drawing on our imagination; we are seeking instead to listen to the words of Holy Scripture, in which God himself tells us the truth about himself. For God our Creator, whom we could never have discovered by an exercise of imagination, has revealed himself. He has talked. He has spoken through many human agents and messengers – and supremely through his Son, our Lord Jesus Christ. . . . in the Bible, God's "public record," as Calvin called it, we find God speaking repeatedly about his jealousy.[37]

"For you shall worship no other god, for the Lord, whose name is Jealous, is a jealous God" (Exodus 34:14). In this clear declaration from the mouth of God, we see that he embraces jealousy as a means of self-identification. Elsewhere we read, ". . . I will be jealous for my holy name" (Ezekiel 39:25). After instructing the Israelites regarding the severity of idolatry, Moses declares, "For the Lord your God is a consuming fire, a jealous God" (Deuteronomy 4:24). The Scriptures are abundantly clear that God is indeed a jealous God and has openly declared himself to be so. The reason why there is no shame or sin in his testimony about himself is that there is no greater being anywhere. He alone, as the sovereign creator of all things, is worthy of praise and adoration. God's perfect nature demands worship and abhors idolatry (see Romans 1:18-23) since he alone is deserving of such honor. We, as mere creatures, would do well to learn and embrace the heavenly chorus of Revelation 4: "Worthy are you, our Lord and God, to receive glory and honor and power, for you created all things, and by your will they existed and were

---

37 Packer, *Knowing God*, pp. 167-168.

created" (Revelation 4:11). God zealously protects his own honor since he alone is worthy of it. Were he to tolerate the adoration of lesser beings, he would cease to be holy since he has created all things for his glory: "The heavens declare the glory of God, and the sky above proclaims his handiwork" (Psalm 19:1). His position as supreme ruler is the fuel that drives the sanctions of the first and second commandments:

> You shall have no other gods before me. You shall not make for yourself a carved image, or any likeness of anything that is in heaven above, or that is in the earth beneath, or that is in the water under the earth. You shall not bow down to them or serve them, for I the Lord your God am a jealous God . . . (Exodus 20:3-5)

In these commands, God is not competing with other deities of equal status for the affection and attention of his worshipers. He is the *only* God. The Lord himself illustrated this clearly when he shouted: "Be gone, Satan! For it is written, 'You shall worship the Lord your God and him only shall you serve'" (Matthew 4:10).

Another aspect of God's jealousy that must be considered is that of his love for his people. Regarding God's jealous love, Packer writes:

> The Old Testament regards God's covenant as his marriage with Israel, carrying with it a demand for unqualified love and loyalty. The worship of idols, and all compromising relations with non-Israelite idolaters, constituted disobedience and unfaithfulness, which God saw as spiritual adultery, provoking him to jealousy and vengeance. . . And it is in light of God's overall plan for his world that his jealousy must, in the last analysis, be understood. For God's ultimate objective, as the Bible declares it, is threefold — to vindicate his rule and

righteousness by showing his sovereignty in judgment upon sin; to ransom and redeem his chosen people; and to be loved and praised by them for his glorious acts of love and self-vindication. God seeks what we should seek – his glory, in and through men – and it is for the securing of this end, ultimately, that he is jealous.

In *Song of Solomon*, we see a poignant description of love's jealousy: ". . . for love is strong as death, jealousy is fierce as the grave. Its flashes are flashes of fire, the very flame of the Lord" (Song of Solomon 8:6). God is and must be infinitely jealous for his holy name's sake. He is also rightly jealous for the worship of his people. If we balk at this notion, it is only a manifestation of our low view of God. We must, by his grace, embrace the Puritan view: "Thou hast brought me to the valley of vision, where I live in the depths but see thee in the heights; hemmed in by mountains of sin I behold thy glory."[38]

---

38 Bennett, *The Valley of Vision*, p. xxiv.

✝

CHAPTER FIFTEEN

The God Who Hates Sin (His Wrath)

If I love children, I must hate abortion.[39] This analogy may seem needlessly provocative, but I assure you it is completely appropriate in regards to the topic at hand. The inherent logic is simple and, in my opinion, self-evident: If I love and care for the well-being, safety, and overall nurture of children, then the logical outflow is that I *must* abhor the mutilation and murder of children. Likewise, since God is the pinnacle of perfection, holy in all his attributes, zealously devoted to his own honor, and in love with all that is good (that which conforms to his very nature), he must hate that which is in opposition to his nature and holy name. Although the earnest seeker of teaching on the holy wrath of God may search in vain in the milieu of today's Christian culture, he need only turn to the Scriptures to find strikingly clear affirmations of God's righteous wrath toward sin.

Christ's words to Nicodemus found in John 3:16 are iconic, though rarely are his words, spoken twenty verses later, uttered or expounded upon: "Whoever believes in the Son has eternal life; whoever does not obey the Son shall not see life, but the *wrath* of God remains on him"

---

39   I first heard this analogy from Brother Paul Washer of HeartCry Mission Society.

(John 3:36, emphasis added). Ironically, the verse that many Christians and even non-Christians have memorized and display on various items of merchandise as a signpost of God's love is, contextually, the foundation for a verse that clearly teaches that God experiences holy wrath toward the reprobate. Paul boldly declares that "the wrath of God is revealed from heaven against all ungodliness and unrighteousness of men, who by their unrighteousness suppress the truth" (Romans 1:18). In the book of Exodus, we see the anger of God kindled against the gross idolatry of the Israelites: "And the Lord said to Moses, 'I have seen this people, and behold, it is a stiff-necked people. Now therefore let me alone, that my wrath may burn hot against them and I may consume them, in order that I may make a great nation of you'" (Exodus 32:9-10). To the naysayer that objects to the idea of God being angry, wrathful, or capable of hate, the Scriptures themselves rise up and denounce him. God *hates* sin. It is because of sin that God is "a God who feels indignation [righteous anger] every day" (Psalm 7:11). In light of the many Scriptures that attest to the reality of God's righteous anger, Pink states:

> Yes, many there are who turn away from a vision of God's wrath as though they were called to look upon some blotch in the Divine character or some blot upon the Divine government. But what saith the Scriptures? As we turn to them we find that God has made no attempt to conceal the facts concerning his wrath. *He is not ashamed to make it known that vengeance and fury belong to him.* . . . A study of the concordance will show that there are *more* references in Scripture to the anger, fury, and wrath of God, than there are to his love and tenderness. Because God is holy, he hates all sin; and because he hates all sin, his anger burns against the sinner (Ps. 7:11).[40]

---

40 Pink, *The Attributes of God*, pp. 105-106.

Such weighty truth demands that we acknowledge the perfection of God's wrath as an attribute equal, and not subordinate, to his holiness. "Therefore I swore in my wrath, 'They shall not enter my rest'" (Psalm 95:11). In this passage, the Lord swears an oath by his *wrath*. If his righteous anger against sin were in any way imperfect, his oath would amount to nothing more than confusing rhetoric. The reality, however, is that God's holy wrath is such that he calls upon it as aptly as he does his other attributes. Furthermore, this divine manifestation of justice against sin should cause the true Christian to weep with joy, sing with thanksgiving, serve with compassion, and preach with fiery zeal. It is against the backdrop of the dreadful reality of God's righteous anger that we savor the words of Paul: "Since, therefore, we have now been justified by his blood, much more shall we be saved by him from the wrath of God" (Romans 5:9). Much will be said of this glorious reality in later chapters, though it is imperative at this point that the reader's eyes, heart, and affection be turned toward the wrath-bearer:

> My Father, enlarge my heart, warm my affections, open my lips, supply words that proclaim "Love lustres at Calvary." There grace removes my burdens and heaps them on thy Son, made a transgressor, a curse, and sin for me; There the word of thy justice smote the man, thy fellow; There thy infinite attributes were magnified, and infinite atonement was made; There infinite punishment was due, and infinite punishment was endured. . . . O Father, who spared not thine only Son that thou mightest spare me, All this transfer thy love designed and accomplished; help me to adore thee by lips and life.[41]

---

41   Bennett, *The Valley of Vision*, pp. 76-77.

✝

◈ PART TWO ◈

THE WALKING DEAD –
MAN'S FALLEN CONDITION

"Against you, you only, have I sinned and done what is evil in your sight, so that you may be justified in your words and blameless in your judgment. Behold, I was brought forth in iniquity, and in sin did my mother conceive me" (Psalm 51:4-5).

"And you were *dead* in the trespasses and sins in which you once walked, following the course of this world, following the prince of the power of the air, the spirit that is now at work in the sons of disobedience – among whom we all once lived in the passions of our flesh, carrying out the desires of the body and the mind, and were by nature children of wrath, like the rest of mankind" (Ephesians 2:1-3, emphasis added).

Chapter Sixteen

Man Created in the Image of God (Imago Dei)

In the Latin tongue, *Imago Dei* means "the image of God." The reality of this scriptural truth is the basis for the abhorrence of ideologies that reduce man to a mere animal. On the sixth day of creation, God crowned his creation with its intended vice-regent: man. The witness of Scripture states:

> Then God said, "Let us make man in our image, after our likeness. And let them have dominion over the fish of the sea and over the birds of the heavens and over the livestock and over all the earth and over every creeping thing that creeps on the earth." So God created man in his own image, in the image of God he created him; male and female he created them" (Genesis 1:26-27).

If one were to resist and say that the Genesis account is mere poetry that teaches a moral truth, the affirmation of its historicity is affirmed by the lips of the Savior himself: "Have you not read that he who created them from the beginning made them male and female . . ." (Matthew 19:4). Though not identical to God (nothing is identical to God), man was made like God. A similar idea is found later in Genesis at the birth of Seth: "When Adam had lived 130 years, he fathered a son in his own *likeness*, after his *image*, and named him Seth" (Genesis 5:3, emphasis added). Though Seth was a distinct person, he was certainly like his father in many ways. To press further beyond the bounds of the revelation of Scripture and hypothesize as to the exact ways in which man is like God is tedious and fraught with peril. Sufficed to say, man was made in the image of God and was called to perfect, sinless communion with his creator.

There is a vastly important, pride-killing reality embedded in the record of creation. Since man was created, he was also accountable to the creator. Writing on the original state of man, Greg Gilbert states:

> When God created human beings, his intention was that they would live under his righteous rule in perfect joy, worshipping him, obeying him, and thereby living in unbroken fellowship with him. . . . he created man and woman in his own image, meaning that they were to be like him, to be in relationship with him, and to declare his glory to the world. Further, God had a job for humans to do. They were to be his vice-regents, ruling his world under him. "Be fruitful and multiply," God told them, "and fill the earth and subdue it and have dominion over the fish of the sea and over the birds of the heavens and over every living thing that moves on the earth" (Genesis 1:28).[42]

What an insult it is for man to devise philosophies that degrade his status to that of the very animals over which he was given authority. Though it may be chic to sneer at the idea that man was made in God's image, the bloody witness of history testifies to the consequences of

---

42   Greg Gilbert, *What is the Gospel?* (Wheaton, IL: Crossway, 2010), p. 48.

viewing man as a mere cosmic accident with no inherent worth. Scripture states, "Whoever sheds the blood of man, by man shall his blood be shed, for God made man in his own image" (Genesis 9:6). Likewise, the witness of the New Testament declares: "But no human being can tame the tongue. It is a restless evil, full of deadly poison. With it we bless our Lord and Father, and with it we curse people who are made in the likeness of God" (James 3:8-9).

Perhaps the most poignant vision afforded to us by the examination of man's creation is the perfect communion to which he was originally called to enjoy with God Almighty. It is a touching scene indeed to imagine our first parent (Adam) communing with God as the animals were being named: "Now out of the ground the Lord God had formed every beast of the field and every bird of the heavens and brought them to the man to see what he would call them. And whatever the man called every living creature, that was its name" (Genesis 2:19). What a beautiful picture of sinless communion between a loving creator and his beloved creation.

CHAPTER SEVENTEEN

Man Ushers Death Into the World (Sin, Guilt, and Depravity)

"Therefore, just as sin came into the world through one man, and death through sin, and so death spread to all men because all sinned" (Romans 5:12). As these words of Paul ring out with hurricane force, we exit the garden of sweet communion and enter the wilderness of destitution. Having examined and savored the fellowship that existed between man and God in the garden, we must also examine Scripture's account of man's fall into sin, depravity, and death. Few other Christian doctrines evoke such rancor from its opponents than does the doctrine of man's inherited guilt and depravity. Protest as we may, the Scriptures are crushingly clear. After warning Adam not to eat of the tree of the knowledge of good and evil (see Genesis 2:16-17), the Lord creates a helper for him (Eve). As Genesis chapter three unfolds, the demise of Adam, Eve, and their offspring for thousands of generations unfolds as well:

> He [Satan] said to the woman, "Did God actually say, 'You shall not eat of any tree in the garden'?" . . . But the serpent said to the woman, "You will not surely die.

For God knows that when you eat of it your eyes will be opened, and you will be like God, knowing good and evil." So when the woman saw that the tree was good for food, and that it was a delight to the eyes, and that the tree was to be desired to make one wise, she took of its fruit and ate, and she also gave some to her husband who was with her, and he ate. Then the eyes of both were opened, and they knew that they were naked. And they sewed fig leaves together and made themselves loincloths. And they heard the sound of the Lord God walking in the garden in the cool of the day, and the man and his wife hid themselves from the presence of the Lord God among the trees of the garden (Genesis 3:1, 4-8).

Having been warned in vivid, unveiled terms, the man and woman made a conscious decision to rebel against their loving, righteous, holy, and ultimately praiseworthy creator. As their teeth penetrated the fruit, one could say that all creation cried, "Treason!" In his classic *Institutes of the Christian Religion*, John Calvin states:

> The prohibition to touch the tree of the knowledge of good and evil was a trial of obedience, that Adam, observing it, might prove his willing submission to the command of God. For the very term shows the end of the precept to have been to keep him contented with his lot, and not allow him arrogantly to aspire beyond it. . . . the first man revolted against the authority of God, not only in allowing himself to be ensnared by the wiles of the devil, but also by despising the truth, and turning aside to lies. Assuredly, when the word of God is despised, all reverence for him is gone. . . . After the heavenly image in man was effaced, he not only was himself

punished by a withdrawal of the ornaments in which he had been arrayed, i.e., wisdom, virtue, justice, truth, and holiness, and by the substitution in their place of those dire pests, blindness, impotence, vanity, impurity, and unrighteousness, but he involved his posterity also, and plunged them in the same wretchedness. This is the hereditary corruption to which early Christian writers gave the name of original sin, meaning by the term the depravation of a nature formerly good and pure.[43]

Let the record show that mankind's first parents were not duped but rather made an informed and willing decision to rebel against divine revelation and embrace a debasing lie. The Lord, being righteous, holy, and just, exacted the punishment due to the crime of high treason (see Genesis 3:14-19).

Adam, as the head or representative of the human race, passed on his corrupted nature to his offspring who were born in his likeness. We, as sons and daughters of Adam, inherit our father's guilt and corruption, which manifest in diverse and manifold ways from the earliest days of our infancy to our final breath. Of man's fallen nature, Charles Leiter writes:

> Sin is universal in the human race. . . . You and I may not have met each other, but of one thing we can be certain even before our introduction – both of us are sinners. Every man, woman, and child on the face of the earth, no matter how old or how young, is a sinner. Even small children, when allowed to go their own way, are capable of the most exquisite cruelties to animals and to one another. Race and nationality likewise offer no immunity from sin; the most cultured of nations are just as capable of genocide as

---

43 Calvin, *Institutes*, pp. 149-150.

the most barbaric. The gas chambers of the "civilized" are merely sophisticated forms of the machetes wielded by the "uncivilized." ... The question is not whether men have had an opportunity to "accept Jesus." The question is whether they have had an opportunity to mistreat the missionary and reject his message – for, apart from the special working of the Holy Spirit, that is what they will surely do.[44]

And that together, Adam and the Scriptures declare that "All we like sheep have gone astray; we have turned – every one – to his own way" (Isaiah 53:6). The desire for autonomy and self-governance is the vile thread that runs from Eden through the hearts of every human that has walked the sod of this earth. David knew this to be sickeningly true when he cried, "Behold, I was brought forth in iniquity, and in sin did my mother conceive me" (Psalm 51:5).

Sin means to fall short of God's standard. Paul describes it this way: "For all have sinned and *fall short* of the glory of God" (Romans 3:23, emphasis added). Lest we misunderstand the great apostle, we must examine another text in order to illustrate that *falling short* is not the result of man's earnest attempts to please the Lord of glory, but is the outflow of his wicked heart:

> And you were dead in the trespasses and sins in which you once walked, following the course of this world, following the prince of the power of the air [Satan], the spirit that is now at work in the sons of disobedience – among whom we all once lived in the passions of our flesh, carrying out the desires of the body and the mind, *and were by nature children of wrath*, like the rest of mankind (Ephesians 2:1-3, emphasis added).

---

44   Charles Leiter, *Justification and Regeneration* (Hannibal, MO: Granted Ministries Press, 2009), pp. 17-18.

The Lord himself indicts all mankind for their sinful actions as well as their sinful nature:

> And he said, "What comes out of a person is what defiles him. For from within, out of the heart of man, come evil thoughts, sexual immorality, theft, murder, adultery, coveting, wickedness, deceit, sensuality, envy, slander, pride, foolishness. All these evils come from within, and they defile a person" (Mark 7:20-23).

Jeremiah likewise testifies that the "heart is deceitful above all things, and desperately sick" (Jeremiah 17:9). In an age in which self-empowerment, vanity, and pride are applauded vices, the teaching of man's fallen nature is often seen as archaic, simplistic, naive, hurtful, obnoxious, shocking, and distasteful. In the face of such opposition, however, the clear testimony of Scripture and experience declares that man is unholy, bent on autonomy, and unable to fulfill the righteous demands of God's law (see Exodus 20:1-17). In his penetrating book, *The Plight of Man and the Power of God*, Martyn Lloyd-Jones states:

> Men resent the very idea of God and feel that it means and implies that their liberty is somehow curtailed. They believe that they are fit to be "master of their fate and captains of their souls," and believing that, they demand the right to manage themselves in their own way and to live their own lives. They refuse to worship and glorify God. They disown Him and turn their backs upon Him and say that they do not need Him. They renounce His way of life and shake off what they regard as the bondage and serfdom of religion and a life controlled by God. He confuses lawlessness and license with freedom; he is a rebel against God and refuses to glorify God.[45]

---

45   Martyn Lloyd-Jones, *The Plight of Man and the Power of God* (Ross-Shire, Great Britain: Christian Focus Publications, Ltd., 2010), p. 27.

Such an allegation might seem like empty rhetoric to the reader who does not have a biblical understanding of the nature of God. If God is not holy, righteous, omnipotent, or just, then man's supposed gross violations of God's law would be petty misdemeanors worthy of an approving wink from a god who is no more than a cosmic grandpa. This, as we have seen in the preceding chapters, is far from being the case. The weightiness of sin causes many attention-seeking, man-pleasing ministers to take the edge off the Bible's clear teaching on the matter. In so doing, the holiness of God is grossly decreased and the sinfulness of man is minimized while his supposed inner goodness is wrongly increased. In light of this woefully common practice, Paul Washer states:

> Although the subject of sin is somewhat out of vogue, even in some evangelical circles, any honest consideration of Scripture as it relates to contemporary culture will demonstrate that there is still a need to make much of sin. The need for clear communication about sin is acute since we live in a generation born in and cultivated by sin. We are a people that drinks down iniquity like water, and cannot discern our fallen condition any more than a fish can know that it is wet. Because of this, we must endeavor to rediscover a biblical view of sin and the sinfulness of man. Our understanding of God and the gospel depends on it. . . . Men have only one problem: they are under the wrath of God because of their sin.[46]

Man's rebellion against his creator has never abated, and it rages on to this day. When men are confronted with the Bible's witness about their fallen condition, they kick and scratch in an effort to escape the indictment that stands against them. Paul tells us that "the wrath of God

---

46 Paul Washer, *The Gospel's Power and Message* (Grand Rapids, MI: Reformation Heritage Books, 2012), p. 75.

is revealed from heaven against all ungodliness and unrighteousness of men, who by their unrighteousness suppress the truth" (Romans 1:18). Without a sovereign act of grace on the part of his creator, man's corrupt heart longs to silence the voice of conscience that condemns it: "As it is written, 'None is righteous, no, not one; no one understands; *no one seeks for God'*" (Romans 3:10-11, emphasis added). Leiter comments on fallen man's gnawing internal awareness that sin deserves punishment: "But no matter how men may try to suppress it, there is still an indelible knowledge in the human heart that *right* and *wrong* are real, that men are *responsible* for their wrongdoing, and that sin *deserves* to be punished."[47] With the candid introspection that has become a hallmark of their writings, one Puritan brother states it this way:

> It is a good day to me when thou givest me a glimpse of myself; Sin is my greatest evil, but thou art my greatest good; I have cause to loathe myself, and not to seek self-honour, for no one desires to commend his own dunghill. My country, family, church fare worse because of my sins, for sinners bring judgment in thinking sins are small, or that God is not angry with them. Let me not take other good men as my example, and think I am good because I am like them, For all good men are not so good as thou desirest, are not always consistent, do not always follow holiness, do not feel eternal good in sore affliction.[48]

---

47 Leiter, *Justification and Regeneration*, p. 23.

48 Bennett, *The Valley of Vision*, p. 122.

CHAPTER EIGHTEEN

Man and the Ultimate Consequences
of Sin (Eternal Punishment)

In light of man's rebellion, we must consider God's appropriate response as the *ultimately* offended party. Can God continue to be holy, blameless, righteous, and just if he gives an approving nod to mutinous rebels in his kingdom? If God were to act judiciously against them, what would it look like? There is an increasing number of books, articles, and sermons being put forth in favor of an upheaval of the traditional view of God's punishment of sinners. Would a loving God punish one of his beloved creatures? Is the God of the New Testament really as cantankerous as the God of the Old Testament? Why would God command us to arbitrarily forgive and yet not exercise forgiveness in the same manner? These and other related questions have been raised regarding the doctrine of eternal punishment. Not only does fallen man not see himself as heinous before a holy and righteous God, he also vomits at the idea of being punished for his crimes. To complicate the matter further, opponents of eternal punishment cite Scripture, often with wanton disregard for context, in order to make a case for a loving God that would never punish his creatures.

The glaring truth of the matter is that Jesus taught us more about hell and God's wrath toward sin than any of his forerunners. Teaching in parabolic fashion regarding his return, Jesus says, "The master of that servant will come on a day when he does not expect him and at an hour he does not know and will cut him in pieces and put him with the hypocrites. In that place there will be weeping and gnashing of teeth" (Matthew 24:50-51). Jesus also exhorts his followers with this shocking revelation: "And do not fear those who kill the body but cannot kill the soul. Rather fear him who can destroy both soul and body in hell" (Matthew 10:28). Jesus, as God incarnate, reveals his holy love as well as his holy wrath against sin. Of the righteous indignation of God toward sinners, Leiter writes:

> The whole moral fabric of the universe would collapse if He *did not* put you in hell. It is in this context that the Bible speaks of the "wrath of God." God's wrath is not a temporary loss of self-control or a selfish fit of emotion. It is his holy, white-hot hatred of sin, the reaction and revulsion of His holy nature against all that is evil. God's wrath is tied in directly with His justice. It has to do with His righteous determination to punish every sin, to balance the scales of justice, and to make every wrong right.... God's wrath *will* eventually be "poured out"; He is a righteous judge and *will not* allow sin to go unpunished forever.[49]

The testimony of Scripture is exceedingly clear on this matter. God is represented as a righteous judge who is prepared and willing to punish sinners. The modern euphemism that naively declares that *God loves the sinner, but hates the sin* is unbiblical and misleading. Scripture states, "God is a righteous judge, and a God who feels indignation every day. If a man does not repent, God will whet his sword; he has bent and readied his bow" (Psalm 7:11-12). God punishes sinners, not their sins.

---

49 Leiter, *Justification and Regeneration*, p. 23.

The question remains as to the nature of his punishment. Do souls merely cease to exist after certain duration under God's judgment? For insight, we turn to Berkhof who writes:

> The question of the eternity of the future punishment deserves more special consideration, however, because it is frequently denied. It is said that the words used in Scripture for "everlasting" and "eternal" may simply denote an "age" or a "dispensation," or any other long period of time. Now it cannot be doubted that they are so used in some passages, but this does not prove that they always have that limited meaning. It is not the literal meaning of these terms. Whenever they are so used, they are used figuratively, and in such cases their figurative use is generally quite evident from the connection. . . . In Matt. 25:46 the same word describes the duration of both, the bliss of the saints and the penalty of the wicked. If the latter is not, properly speaking, unending, neither is the former; and yet many of those who doubt eternal punishment, do not doubt everlasting bliss.[50]

Though it may be unpopular and offensive to the modern ear, God's wrath against sinners burns forever. Their sinfulness remains and therefore "the wrath of God remains on them" (John 3:36). With penetrating insight into this topic, Washer writes:

> The oft-repeated statement that God is not an angry God is untrue and it cannot offer any real comfort to man! What comfort could be found in a God who is neutral toward evil and demonstrates no indignation against it? How could God be good, loving, or even

---

50   Berkhof, *Systematic Theology*, p. 736.

moral if He did not burn with indignation over the slave trade, Auschwitz, or the slaughter of millions of unborn children in the name of convenience?. . . Can we justify our own indignation toward unrighteousness and all the while deny such a right to God?[51]

Due to his own holiness and justice, God's righteous reaction to sin is proper. Since man is inherently corrupt, the wrath of God burns against him: "you hate all evildoers" (Psalm 5:5). Hell's eternal flame is the manifestation of God's holy wrath against sin. Jesus warns us repeatedly of the place of judicial punishment "where the worm does not die and the fire is not quenched" (Mark 9:48). It is at this point that the gavel of divine justice rightly falls and pronounces judgment against the entirety of mankind, Adam's fallen sons and daughters.

---

51   Washer, *The Gospel's Power and Message*, p. 133.

†

CHAPTER NINETEEN

Man in God's Courtroom (The Dilemma of Proverbs 17:15)

"He who *justifies the wicked* and he who condemns the righteous are both alike an abomination to the Lord" (Proverbs 17:15, emphasis added). In light of the previous chapter's effort to expose God's white-hot wrath against the sinner, we must pause to marvel at the complexity of man's situation. We all stand rightly condemned before a holy God just as Joshua stood before the Lord in filthy garments (see Zechariah 3:1-5). God could have made a sovereign choice to save no one and his character would have remained flawless. The judge of all creation would have been justified and even praised for his righteousness if he had sentenced every son and daughter of Adam to eternal torment. However, the confounding truth of Scripture declares:

> For while we were still weak, at the right time Christ died for the ungodly. For one will scarcely die for a righteous person – though perhaps for a good person one would dare even to die – but God shows his love for us in that

while we were still sinners, Christ died for us. Since, therefore, we have now been *justified by his blood,* much more shall we be saved by him from the wrath of God (Romans 5:6-9, emphasis added).

How, in light of Proverbs 17:15, can defiled sinners be justified without tarnishing the character of God? Of Proverbs 17:15, Leiter offers the following illustration:

> Suppose a father comes home to find his family murdered. After an agonizing chase, he is able to apprehend the murderer. When the criminal finally appears before the judge, he is found to be unquestionably guilty of the crime. But when the time of sentencing comes, the judge makes the following declaration: "This man has committed a horrible crime, but I am a very loving judge and choose to declare him not guilty. In fact, I declare him to be righteous in the sight of the law!" Such a judge would rightly be considered as great a criminal as the offender! He has "justified the wicked" and is "an abomination to the Lord."[52]

A solemn situation demands a solemn and weighty analogy such as this. At this juncture, we should ask with Job: "But how can a man be in the right before God?" (Job 9:2). The answer lies in the proper, biblical definition of *justification.*

Justification is an "instantaneous legal act of God in which he (1) thinks of our sins as forgiven and Christ's righteousness as belonging to us, and (2) declares us to be righteous in his sight."[53] Unlike the wicked judge from the analogy, God does not merely overlook sin in order to

---

52 Leiter, *Justification and Regeneration*, p. 25.

53 Grudem, *Systematic Theology*, p. 1246.

express his love. If he were to do so, he would cease to be righteous. And yet the resounding witness of Scripture is that God justifies wicked men. The answer to the dilemma of Proverbs 17:15, according to our definition, is the wrath-bearing sacrifice of Christ. Of this glorious reality, Leiter exults:

> There is only one answer to the dilemma. Someone has to pay for the sinner's sins. Justice must be satisfied. Either it will be satisfied by the sinner's own suffering forever in hell, or it must be satisfied by someone else on the sinner's behalf. Wonder of wonders! That 'Someone' has come![54]

God vindicated his holy name by publically displaying his Son at the epicenter of the religious world. Paul clarifies how a holy God could show favor to rebels who:

> . . . are justified by his grace as a gift, through the redemption that is in Christ Jesus, whom God put forward as a propitiation by his blood, to be received by faith. This was to show God's righteousness, because in his divine forbearance he had passed over former sins. *It was to show his righteousness at the present time, so that he might be just and the justifier of the one who has faith in Jesus* (Romans 3:24-26, emphasis added).

The sinless sacrifice of the Son of God (see John 1:29) is the resounding answer regarding God's abhorrence of those who wrongly pardon the guilty and his bestowal of grace upon such people. God does not and cannot merely *live and let live*. As seen in his attributes, his very nature demands that his holy name be defended and honored. The cross

---

54 Leiter, *Justification and Regeneration*, p. 26.

of Christ stands as a lighthouse on a high, rocky crag that illuminates the mystery of God's redemptive plan. Man has transgressed the holy law of his holy, sovereign creator, and justice must be served. Scripture responds by boldly declaring: "But when the fullness of time had come, God sent forth his Son, born of woman, born under the law, to redeem those who were under the law, so that we might receive adoption as sons" (Galatians 4:4-5). In the sacrifice of Christ, the dilemma is gloriously resolved.

✝

⤖ PART THREE ⤖

God in Action –
His Response to
Man's Plight

"Surely he has borne our griefs and carried our sorrows; yet we esteemed him stricken, smitten by God and afflicted. But he was wounded for our transgressions; he was crushed for our iniquities; upon him was the chastisement that brought us peace, and with his stripes we are healed" (Isaiah 53:4-5).

"In this is love, not that we have loved God but that he loved us and sent his Son to be the propitiation for our sins" (1 John 4:10).

✝

CHAPTER TWENTY

Christ Fulfills the Law (His Perfect Life as the God-Man)

"For whoever keeps the whole law but fails in one point has become accountable for all of it" (James 2:10). Apart from the grace of God in Christ, man has no hope. The divine law written on the stone tablets of Sinai and on our hearts proves to be an unyielding prosecutor. David declared that the "law of the Lord is perfect" (Psalm 19:7). Another word for perfect in this verse is *blameless*. When we speak of the law of God condemning us, we cannot shake a closed fist in the direction of the lawgiver as if his law were an underhanded, unnecessary, or imperfect thing. The fault lies squarely on our shoulders, the fallen sons and daughters of Adam. The law serves to manifest the righteousness of God in his judgments against depraved, rebellious men:

> Now we know that whatever the law says it speaks to those who are under the law, so that every mouth may be stopped, and the whole world may be held accountable to God. For by works of the law no human being will be justified in his sight, since through the law comes knowledge of sin (Romans 3:19-20).

On the Day of Judgment, the law of God will expose the sinful, God-hating inclinations of the hearts of men (see Jeremiah 17:9) so much so that "every mouth may be stopped." God's holy name will be vindicated since unbelieving men will be found "without excuse" (Romans 1:20). In light of such devastating realities, we may all stand together and ask, "Brothers, what shall we do?" (Acts 2:37).

Not only does the sacrifice and resurrection of Jesus Christ answer our question, his *sinless life* responds with an equally sweet chorus of grace. Could the omnipotent God of creation send Christ to earth as a fully grown man and place him on the cross without delay? What then does this say about the efficacious nature of his thirty-three years on earth? First, the redemption of fallen humanity required that the sacrifice for its transgressions of God's law be of like kind. Of the Old Testament's system of continuous animal sacrifices, the writer of Hebrews states, "For it is impossible for the blood of bulls and goats to take away sins" (Hebrews 10:4). The river of blood that flows through the pages of the Old Testament is swallowed up by the cross of Christ. Of Jesus, John declares, "And the Word became flesh and dwelt among us" (John 1:14). Likewise, the writer of Hebrews says, "Since therefore the children share in flesh and blood, he himself likewise partook of the same things, that through death he might destroy the one who has the power of death, that is, the Devil" (Hebrews 2:14). Jesus suffered as a man in order to redeem men. Secondly, the life of Christ is gloriously significant because it was the *only* human life that perfectly conformed to the will of God. Not only does fallen man need his sin removed, he also needs righteousness to be credited to him. The prophet Zechariah, in his vision of Joshua the high priest, offers a stunningly beautiful picture of the removal of sin and the imputation (to reckon something as belonging to someone) of righteousness:

Now Joshua was standing before the angel, clothed with

filthy garments. And the angel said to those who were standing before him, 'Remove the filthy garments from him.' And to him he said, 'Behold, I have taken your iniquity away from you, and I will clothe you with pure vestments (Zechariah 3:3-4).

In this vision of the courtroom of the Almighty, we may rightly identify with Joshua. As he stands condemned, clothed in his own hellish filth, the Lord himself removes his stained garments and imputes righteousness to him. The perfect life of Christ, when imputed to sinners, clothes them in a spotless gown of righteousness. In God's gracious wisdom, we not only have our sins removed, we have merit credited to our account by the law-keeping, God-pleasing life of Jesus. Jesus Christ alone can boldly declare: "I *always* do the things that are pleasing to him [God the Father]" (John 8:29, emphasis added). Jesus Christ alone can boldly declare: "Do not think that I have come to abolish the Law or the Prophets; I have not come to abolish them but to *fulfill* them" (Matthew 5:17, emphasis added). Christ, as a man, fulfilled the demands of the law for his helpless bride.

The deep mystery of the nature of Christ as the God-man is too precious to be trifled with by mere mortals. Nonetheless, the Scriptures declare the stunning reality of God's love in that God suffered for his people. Rejoicing over the truth of Christ's divinity, Washer writes:

The One who was nailed to the cross of Calvary was God, and the life He gave for the sake of His people was of infinite worth. The One who hung upon the tree was a man whose perfect obedience to the law of God gave merit to His sacrifice and provided a perfect righteousness to be imputed to His people. Therefore, we answer the skeptic's question of how the one can pay for the many by pointing to Jesus Christ, who was able to redeem a nearly countless multitude of men because of his infinite worth as God and His perfect obedience as Man. Regarding the deity of Jesus Christ, we must again affirm that He was God in the very strictest and most complete use of the term. . . . If there had been a sinless man or angel without blame who had been willing to die, his death would not have availed against our sin. . . . Our salvation required a sacrifice of infinite value, and "our great God and Savior Jesus Christ" has such value.[55]

Glory of glories! When we cast our eyes to the bloody cross of Calvary, we see hanging there a man who fulfilled the demands of God's holy law on behalf of his beloved. In the same glimpse, our eyes drink in the vision of the bruised body of God incarnate who is the "Lamb of God, who takes away the sin of the world" (John 1:29). Christ's deity makes his sacrifice alone worthy of infinite value. It is at the contemplation of this perfect sacrifice that Peter explodes with praise:

> Knowing that you were ransomed from the futile ways inherited from your forefathers, not with perishable things such as silver or gold, but with the precious blood of Christ, like that of a lamb without blemish or spot. He was foreknown before the foundation of the world but was made manifest in the last times for the sake of you who through him are believers in God, who raised him from the dead and gave him glory, so that your faith and hope are in God (1 Peter 1:18-21).

---

55 Washer, *The Gospel's Power and Message*, pp. 171-172.

CHAPTER TWENTY-ONE

Christ Takes Our Place
(Substitutionary Atonement)

Though we have examined the life of Christ in regards to his necessary humanity and deity, we now continue our efforts of mining heavenly gold from the hillside of Golgotha. In an age in which the gospel has been reduced to a formula, a man-centered "plan of salvation" in which the proselyte is given cursory facts about man's depravity and Christ's atoning death, it is our duty and joy to drill deeper into the Word of God in order that the oil of gladness might spring up. The work of Christ on the cross as the sacrificial Lamb of God who died in lieu of his church (which consisted of hateful sinners) is something "into which angels long to look" (1 Peter 1:12).

Substitutionary atonement (as well as *vicarious atonement* or *penal substitution*) combines two terms to make a whole. *Substitution* refers to Christ's act of willingly bearing the penalty of sin for his people:

> Surely he has borne *our* griefs and carried *our* sorrows, yet we esteemed him stricken, smitten by God, and afflicted. But he was wounded for *our* transgressions; he was crushed for *our* iniquities; upon him was the

chastisement that brought us peace, and with his stripes
we are healed (Isaiah 53:4-5, emphasis added).

Clearly the Messiah suffered in place of his people. This fact alone, that the King of kings would suffer the punishment rightly due to his rebellious subjects, should cause us to weep in awestruck wonder. *Atonement* refers to the work accomplished by Christ in his life, death, and resurrection. In short, substitutionary atonement refers to the salvation wrought by Christ by standing in the place of judgment for his people: "For our sake he made him to be sin who knew no sin, so that in him we might become the righteousness of God" (2 Corinthians 5:21).

Perhaps the most vivid illustration of substitutionary atonement appears in the account of Abraham's offering of Isaac upon the altar. In Genesis twenty-two, God commanded Abraham saying, "Take your son, your only son Isaac, whom you love, and go to the land of Moriah, and offer him there as a burnt offering on one of the mountains of which I shall tell you" (Genesis 22:2). The language is striking and calculated: God was teaching a deeper, more glorious lesson by commanding the old man to destroy the son of promise. As the heavy-hearted father drew back the blade, the Lord called out to him and said:

> Do not lay your hand on the boy or do anything to him,
> for now I know that you fear God, seeing that you have
> not withheld your son, your only son, from me." And
> Abraham lifted up his eyes and looked, and behold,
> behind him was a ram, caught in a thicket by his horns.
> And Abraham went and took the ram and offered it up
> as a burnt offering instead of his son. So Abraham called
> the name of that place, "The Lord will provide"; as it is
> said to this day, "On the mount of the Lord it shall be
> provided" (Genesis 22:12).

The Lord did indeed provide a Lamb. Many generations later, the Lamb of God was offered on the mount of Calvary: "For God so loved the world, that he gave his only Son, that whoever believes in him should not perish but have eternal life" (John 3:16). If this magnificent exchange, Spurgeon exposes the shocking truth of the matter:

> I do not think I can preach more, for a faintness has come over me, nor is there need for more if you will but chew the cud of this one precious truth: Jesus is the Lamb which God provided, and He is the Lamb, which God himself presented at the altar. Yet, I must rouse myself to say a little more. Who was it that sacrificed the Lamb of God? Who was the priest on that dread day? Who was it that bruised him? Who put him to grief? Who caused him the direst pang of all when he cried, "Why hast thou forsaken me" Was it not the Father Himself? This was one point in the hardness of Abraham's test – "Take now your son, thine only son Isaac, whom thou lovest, and offer him for a sacrifice." He must himself officiate at the sacrifice. This the great Father did! He is the Lamb, the Lamb of God.[56]

The unlearned might cry, "What kind of God would do such a thing?" In light of man's innate rebellion against his creator, the provision of God's Lamb is not only profoundly amazing, it is also profoundly confusing. The Bible tells us as much when it says, "The natural person does not accept the things of the Spirit of God, for they are folly to him, and he is not able to understand them because they are spiritually discerned" (1 Corinthians 2:14). When we look to Christ as he hangs on his cross, we see the glory of God's Lamb "who takes away the sin of the world" (John 1:29). Like Joshua in Zechariah chapter three, we stood

---

56 Spurgeon, *Spurgeon Gold*, pp. 46-47.

before the bar of God's righteous judgment as condemned sinners clothed in the filthy, odious rags of their iniquities. Satan, the accuser, brought a strong case against us. All of creation cried out for our condemnation. It is in the midst of this heavenly court that we join John in his vision on Patmos: "And between the throne and the four living creatures and among the elders I saw a Lamb standing, as though it had been slain, with seven horns and seven eyes, which are the seven spirits of God sent out into all the earth" (Revelation 5:6). The ram caught in the thicket was a mere shadow of the Lamb who offered himself on behalf of his beloved church. Of Christ, as the divine substitute, Washer writes:

> The curtain draws to a close on a slain Son, a crucified Messiah, in order to open for hell-worthy sinners. Unlike the account of Isaac, there was no ram to die in His place. He is the Lamb who died for the sins of the world. He is God's provision for the redemption of His people. He is the fulfillment of that which Isaac and the ram only foreshadowed. In Him, that dreadful Mount called Golgotha is now renamed *YHWH-jireh* or "The Lord will provide."[57]

The substitutionary death of Christ shines like a supernova against the backdrop of man's unworthiness: "For one will scarcely die for a righteous person – though perhaps for a good person would dare even to die – but God shows his love for us in that while we were still sinners, Christ died for us" (Romans 5:7-8). Divine, holy justice demands satisfaction. In the cross of Christ, God's justice was satisfied on behalf of the church, the bride of Christ. I have often told my daughter, "Either daddy goes on the cross or Jesus goes on the cross." In these simple, breathtakingly sweet conversations, I am brought face-to-face with the reality of my station as a man in need of a Savior. Praise be to God, he has provided just that.

---

57 Washer, *The Gospel's Power and Message*, p. 194.

CHAPTER TWENTY-TWO

Christ Endures the Wrath We Deserve (Propitiation)

It is tragic that a word so pregnant with glorious truth should fall out of modern Christian vernacular. Search the Internet or a Christian bookstore and you will be hard-pressed to find a sermon or book that explains that Christ's sacrifice was a *propitiation*. Though some may charge that such large and antiquated terms are unnecessary for the modern follower of Christ, the witness of Scripture, even the most modern translations, says otherwise: "In this is love, not that we have loved God but that he loved us and sent his Son to be the *propitiation* for our sins" (1 John 4:10, emphasis added). In the context of this verse, we see a connection between the perfect love of God for his people and the atoning work of Christ as a *propitiation*. This observation alone, that God's love is in some way linked to the term at hand, should cause us to ponder what the word *propitiation* means and why it is crucial to our understanding of the cross.

Grudem defines propitiation as "a sacrifice that bears God's wrath to the end and in so doing changes God's wrath toward us into favor."[58] In light of the previous chapters' unveiling of God's glorious attributes

---

58 Grudem, *Systematic Theology*, p. 575.

and man's innate corruption, a term that serves to explain how the divine wrath against rebellious sinners can be exhausted so that the undeserving transgressors can receive grace is worthy of our attention and apprehension. It is here that we again turn our attention to Paul's letter to the Romans in which we read of Christ: "Whom God put forward as a propitiation by his blood, to be received by faith. This was to show God's righteousness, because in his divine forbearance he had passed over former sins" (Romans 3:25). Of this passage, Grudem observes: "God had not simply forgiven sin and forgotten about the punishment in generations past. He had forgiven sins and stored up his righteous anger against those sins. But at the cross the fury of all that stored-up wrath against sin was unleashed against God's own Son."[59] Calvin, in his classic commentary on the book of *Romans*, comments on this verse (3:25) by stating:

> . . . Paul refers to the gratuitous mercy of God, in having appointed Christ as our Mediator, that he might appease the Father by the sacrifice of his death: nor is it a small commendation of God's grace that he, of his own good will, sought out a way by which he might remove our curse.[60]

With this in mind, we turn again to Isaiah's prophecy concerning the coming Messiah: "Yet it was the will of the Lord to crush him; he has put him to grief . . ." (Isaiah 53:10). Christ willingly took upon himself the curse of God's righteous indignation on behalf of his people, for he alone, as the God-Man, was able to extinguish it. In so doing, "Christ redeemed us from the curse of the law by becoming a curse for us" (Galatians 3:13). R. C. Sproul makes the following observation about Christ as the divine curse-bearer:

---

59   Ibid.

60   John Calvin, *Calvin's Commentaries Volume XIX: Acts 14 – Romans 16* (Grand Rapids, MI: Baker Publishing Group, 2009), p. 142.

I have heard many sermons about the physical pain of death by crucifixion. I've heard graphic descriptions of the nails and the thorns. Surely the physical agony of crucifixion was a ghastly thing. But there were thousands who died on crosses and may have had more painful deaths than that of Christ. But only one person has ever received the full measure of the curse of God while on a cross. I doubt that Jesus was even aware of the nails and the spear – He was so overwhelmed by the outer darkness. On the cross Jesus was in the reality of hell. He was totally bereft of the grace and the presence of God, utterly separated from all blessedness of the Father. He became a curse for us so that we someday will be able to see the face of God. So that the light of his countenance might fall upon us, God turned his back on His Son. No wonder Christ screamed. He screamed from the depth of his soul. How long did He have to endure it? We don't know, but a second of it would be of infinite value.[61]

Such gloriously profound truth! How then can we relegate such as a word as *propitiation* to the junkyard of antiquated terminology? No, our joy and satisfaction in this life are contingent upon embracing and relishing the truth found in this singular word. For in this word lies the glory of Paul's declaration that "There is therefore now no condemnation for those who are in Christ Jesus" (Romans 8:1). Christ, the wrath-bearing sacrifice, has taken the totality of God's righteous wrath on behalf of his people. It was under the weight of his Father's indignation that he cried, "My God, my God, why have you forsaken me?" (Mark 15:34). Quoting Psalm 22, Christ was teaching his immediate listeners, as well as we who would read them generations later, that the whole of the Psalm was pointing toward his work on the cross:

---

61   R. C. Sproul, *Saved From What?* (Wheaton, IL: Crossway Books, 2002), p. 84.

My God, my God, why have you forsaken me? Why are you so far from saving me, from the words of my groaning? O my God, I cry by day, but you do not answer, and by night, but I find no rest. You are holy, enthroned on the praises of Israel. In you our fathers trusted; they trusted, and you delivered them. To you they cried and were rescued; in you they trusted and were not put to shame. But I am a worm and not a man, scorned by mankind and despised by the people. All who see me mock me; they make mouths at me; they wag their heads; "He trusts in the Lord; let him deliver him; let him rescue him, for he delights in him!" (Psalm 22:1-8).

The sentimental notion that God turned his back on his Son because he could not bear to watch him punished so severely by the Romans is unbiblical and misleading. The shocking, scandalous truth of the cross is this: God poured out his righteous wrath upon his only begotten Son in order that he might declare ungodly rebels to be righteous before him. This is put forth with vivid brilliance in Paul's second letter to the Corinthians: "For our sake he made him to be sin who knew no sin, so that in him we might become the righteousness of God" (2 Corinthians 5:21). Let us look upon the Lamb of God and give thanks to the Father who, according to his sovereign good pleasure, sent his Son who willingly drank "the cup of his wrath . . . to the dregs" (Isaiah 51:17) in order that we guilty sinners might drink from the satisfying springs of grace that flow from the "spiritual Rock . . . and the Rock [is] Christ" (1 Corinthians 10:4).

CHAPTER TWENTY-THREE

Christ Conquered the Grave (His Resurrection)

In his first letter to the Corinthian church, the apostle Paul utters a statement that reveals a potentially fatal flaw in the design of salvation as put forth in the New Testament: "And if Christ has not been raised, your faith is futile and you are still in your sins" (1 Corinthians 15:17). Earlier in the chapter, Paul included the resurrection of Christ in his list of things that were to take primary position in the church:

> For I delivered to you as of first importance what I also received: that Christ died for our sins in accordance with the Scriptures, that he was buried, *that he was raised on the third day in accordance with the Scriptures*, and that he appeared to Cephas, then to the twelve. Then he appeared to more than five hundred brothers at one time, most of whom are still alive, though some have fallen asleep. Then he appeared to James, then to all the apostles. Last of all, as to one untimely born, he appeared also to me (1 Corinthians 15:3-8, emphasis added).

Paul is clear about the potential fatal flaw of verse seventeen. He emphatically declares, with much supporting evidence, that Jesus Christ rose from the dead. It should be noted that the foundation of our faith (according to 1 Corinthians 15:17) is the very thing that earned the apostle Paul the mockery and scorn of the intellectual elite of his day: "Now when they heard of the resurrection of the dead, some mocked. But others said, 'We will hear you again about this'" (Acts 17:32). Christ's humble tomb, unlike the ornate sepulchers of all other deceased spiritual leaders, is still empty. The Scriptures testify that his disciples "found the stone rolled away from the tomb, but when they went in they did not find the body of the Lord Jesus" (Luke 24:2-3). Many people, it may be assumed, would have an easier time accepting Christ's teachings had he simply remained dead. The witness of Scripture, history, and millions of changed lives throughout the world, however, testify that Jesus Christ reigns as the sole victor over the grave!

In addition to the evidence of the empty tomb, many credible witnesses attest to Christ's postmortem appearances. The apostle John unequivocally declares that Christ's resurrection was real and verifiable:

> That which was from the beginning, which we have heard, which we have seen with our eyes, which we looked upon and have touched with our hands, concerning the word of life – the life was made manifest, and we have seen it, and testify to it and proclaim to you the eternal life, which was with the Father and was made manifest to us – that which we have seen and heard we proclaim also to you, so that you too may have fellowship with us; and indeed our fellowship is with the Father and with his Son Jesus Christ. And we are writing these things so that our joy may be complete (1 John 1:1-4).

The apostles never shied away from declaring that Jesus Christ not only died for the sins of his people, but also that he rose "for [their] justification" (Romans 4:25). Other individuals in Scripture were resurrected from the dead: the son of the widow in 1 Kings 17:17-22, numerous saints at Christ's resurrection in Matthew 27:50-53, and Lazarus in John 11:43-44. A number of other passages could be cited, but one common element remains woven into the fabric of each of these accounts that sets them apart from the resurrection of Jesus: all of these resurrected saints went on to die again. Jesus alone is able to declare: "Fear not, I am the first and the last, and the living one. I died, and behold I am alive forevermore, and I have the keys of Death and Hades" (Revelation 1:17-18). Such a glorious proclamation from the lips of the risen Savior resonates in the apostolic preaching of the gospel. Peter, filled with the Holy Spirit on the Day of Pentecost, boldly declared before a multitude: "This Jesus, delivered up according to the definite plan and foreknowledge of God, you crucified and killed by the hands of lawless men. God raised him up, loosing the pangs of death, because it was not possible for him to be held by it" (Acts 2:23-24). The resurrection of Christ has always been the central message to be proclaimed, not debated. The fact that the gospel is "folly to those who are perishing" (1 Corinthians 1:18) should not surprise us. Pointing to the power of God to open the eyes of the skeptical, hardened, and unbelieving, Piper states:

> Like every historical fact, the resurrection of Jesus can be doubted. But when God takes in hand the reliability of the witnesses, the courage of their preaching, the futility of the opposition, the effects of the Gospel, the coherence of the message, the all-embracing sufficiency of the Christian worldview, and the spiritual glory of Jesus Christ – when God takes all this and more in hand, he is able to open the mind of the most resistant skeptic.

When God wakens us from the stupor of unbelief and shines into our mind with "the light of the gospel of the glory of Christ" (2 Corinthians 4:4, 6), what we see, along with the terrible splendor of his suffering, is the grandeur of his resurrection.[62]

Unlike the kings of this world who build kingdoms and dynasties only to succumb to the unyielding sting of death, Christ stands alone in glorious splendor. In light of this, Paul declares:

Therefore God has highly exalted him and bestowed on him the name that is above every name, so that at the name of Jesus every knee should bow, in heaven and on earth and under the earth, and every tongue confess that Jesus Christ is Lord, to the glory of God the Father (Philippians 2:9-11).

---

62 John Piper, *Seeing and Savoring Jesus Christ* (Wheaton, IL: Crossway, 2004), pp. 107-108.

CHAPTER TWENTY-FOUR

Christ Alone is Able to Bring Us to God (Reconciliation)

Due to the fact that reconciliation denotes the breakdown of a relationship, many contented souls would see no need for reconciliation between themselves and God. Many, since the fall of Adam, have been perfectly satisfied to assume that the Lord of Glory is in nowise at odds with them. The idea of needing reconciliation with God is often met with scorn and offense. The truth of Scripture must shine its penetrating light into the darkened hearts of men if they are to awaken to their lot: "For if while we were enemies we were reconciled to God by the death of his Son, much more, now that we are reconciled, shall we be saved by his life" (Romans 5:10). The words of Spurgeon thunder as loudly today as they did many years ago as they candidly and accurately illuminate man's need to be reconciled to God:

> Come down from your high places and see the horrible pit in which you lie by nature. Think of your past lives, I pray you, of those days in which you found pleasure in walking after the flesh. I call on you to remember the sins of your youth,

and your former transgressions of thought, word, and deed. If they are shut out who defile and are defiled, where are you? Where are you? For these sins of ours, though they were committed years ago, are nonetheless sinful today; they are as fresh to God as if we perpetrated them this very moment. You are still red-handed, O sinful man, though your crime was worked some twenty years ago. You are black, O sinner, still, though it be fifty years ago that your chief sin was committed; for time has no bleaching power upon a crimson sin. The guilt of an old offense is as fresh as though it were wrought but yester-morn.[63]

Like the Israelites of Malachi's day, fallen men hear of their need to be reconciled to God and ignorantly ask, "How have we robbed you?" (Malachi 3:8). Thinking too little of their sins and fashioning a view of God that suits their taste, they feel no need of reconciliation since they and their smug idol live in hospitable communion with one another. Here the words of the Lord speaking through Asaph ring out: "These things you have done, and I have been silent; you thought that I was one like yourself . . ." (Psalm 50:21).

In the words of Paul we see a magnificent, life-altering truth bursting forth from the pages of Scripture: ". . . in Christ God was reconciling the world to himself, not counting their trespasses against them, and entrusting to us the message of reconciliation" (2 Corinthians 5:19). Due to man's utter destitution and inability to save himself from the consequences of his sin (see Ephesians 2:1-3), God sovereignly initiates the change of heart and will within the chosen sinner:

I will sprinkle clean water on you, and you shall be clean from all your uncleannesses, and from all your idols I will cleanse you. And I will give you a new heart, and a

---

63 Spurgeon, *Spurgeon Gold*, p. 97.

new spirit I will put within you. And I will remove the heart of stone from your flesh and give you a heart of flesh. And I will put my Spirit within you, and cause you to walk in my statutes and be careful to obey my rules (Ezekiel 36:25-27).

Through the wrath-satisfying, God-glorifying, law-fulfilling, curse-bearing, sin-removing sacrifice of Jesus, God is reconciling sinful rebels to himself. The law of God comes like a hammer to smash the vain hopes and imaginations of men who live at peace with their sins and false views of God. When men are left open and exposed to the condemnation that stands against them in light of God's holiness, the truth of the gospel shines like a sun flare:

For in him all the fullness of God was pleased to dwell, and through him to reconcile to himself all things, whether on earth, or in heaven, making peace by the blood of his cross. And you, who once were alienated and hostile in mind, doing evil deeds, he has now reconciled in his body of flesh by his death, in order to present you holy and blameless and above reproach before him, if indeed you continue in the faith, stable and steadfast, not shifting from the hope of the gospel that you heard, which has been proclaimed in all creation under heaven, and of which I, Paul, became a minister (Colossians 1:19-23).

The Lord of all creation, who could have rightly condemned all of fallen and rebellious humanity, through his Son, is reconciling lost sinners to himself for his own purposes and glory. Christ's sacrifice, resurrection, and ascension to eternal power and glory validate his office as the sole mediator between God and man: "For there is one God, and there is one mediator between God and men, the man Christ Jesus, who gave himself as a ransom for all, which is the testimony given at the proper time" (2 Timothy 2:5-6). Not only did Christ absorb the full force of his Father's wrath against sin, he also mediates between his people and the Father. In an attempt to describe this, a Puritan wrote:

> I have destroyed myself, my nature is defiled, the powers of my soul are degraded; I am vile, miserable, strengthless, but my hope is in thee. . . . Thou hast devised means to rescue me from sin's perdition, to restore me to happiness, honour, safety. I bless thee for the everlasting covenant, for the appointment of a Mediator. I rejoice that he failed not, nor was discouraged, but accomplished the work thou gavest him to do; and said on the cross, "It is finished." I exult in the thought that thy justice is satisfied, thy truth established, thy law magnified, and a foundation is laid for my hope.[64]

Praise the Father for his sovereign initiation of the salvation of lost rebels. Praise the Son for his willing and perfect obedience. Praise the Spirit for his application of the redemption purchased to the hearts and minds of his people. Those who are graciously reconciled may rightly exult in the fact that there is "now no condemnation for those who are in Christ Jesus" (Romans 8:1).

---

64 Bennett, *The Valley of Vision*, pp. 72-73.

CHAPTER TWENTY-FIVE

Christ Sets Us Free from Bondage (Redemption)

The saving work of Jesus Christ saves sinners from bondage. To those who do not feel the rusty chains of sin grinding into their wrists, this message is "folly" (1 Corinthians 1:18). To those who wince at the gnawing pain of enslavement, this message is "the power of God for salvation" (Romans 1:16). To clarify the word *redemption*, we again turn to the insights of Grudem:

> Because we as sinners are in bondage to sin and Satan, we need someone to provide redemption and thereby "redeem" us out of that bondage. When we speak of redemption, the idea of a "ransom" comes into view. A ransom is the price paid to redeem someone from bondage or captivity. . . . If we ask to whom the ransom was paid, we realize that the human analogy of a ransom payment does not fit the atonement of Christ in every detail. Though we were in bondage to sin and Satan, there was no "ransom" paid either to "sin" or to Satan himself, for they did not have power to demand such payment, nor was Satan the one whose holiness was

offended by sin and who required a penalty to be paid for sin. . . . But we hesitate to speak of paying a "ransom" to God the Father, because it was not he who held us in bondage but Satan and our own sins. Therefore at this point the idea of a ransom payment cannot be pressed in every detail. It is sufficient to note that a price was paid (the death of Christ) and the result was that we were "redeemed" from bondage.[65]

Though the ransom analogy should not be applied too broadly, we can wrest from Scripture the consolation of knowing that we who are in Christ by faith are no longer in bondage. Paul tells us that "sin will have no dominion over you, since you are not under the law but under grace" (Romans 6:14). Regarding believers, the great apostle goes on in praising God's sovereign goodness toward ungodly men: "But thanks be to God, that you who were once slaves of sin have become obedient from the heart to the standard of teaching to which you were committed, and, having been set free from sin, have become slaves of righteousness" (Romans 6:17-18). It is against the backdrop of this glorious truth that Paul declares: "For freedom Christ has set us free' stand firm therefore, and do not submit again to a yoke of slavery" (Galatians 5:1). The beautiful irony of Christianity is that we are made free to become slaves of a perfect master. This is *true* freedom.

If any rotten seed of doubt remains concerning the enslavement of unconverted men, the Scriptures clarify the condition of their lot:

And you were dead in the trespasses and sins in which you once walked, following the course of this world, *following the prince of the power of the air*, the spirit that is now at work in the sons of disobedience – among whom we all once lived in the passions of our flesh, carrying out

---

65   Grudem, *Systematic Theology*, p. 580.

the desires of the body and the mind, and were by nature
children of wrath, like the rest of mankind (Ephesians
2:1-3, emphasis added).

Not only do unsaved men heed the yearnings of their flesh, they
also actively and willingly (though perhaps unwittingly) follow Satan.
The Scriptures again bear witness to fallen man's slavish adherence to
the yearnings of his sinful heart: "For we ourselves were once foolish,
disobedient, led astray, *slaves* to various passions and pleasures, passing
our days in malice and envy, hated by others and hating one another"
(Titus 3:3, emphasis added).

It is to the glory of God's marvelous grace that we note that the
next word found in each of the previously cited passages is "but." This
simple three-letter word is then followed by a tsunami of grace that is
constituted by the blood of Christ. In the case of Paul's letter to the
Ephesians: "But God, being rich in mercy, because of the great love with
which he loved us, even when we were dead in our trespasses, made us
alive together with Christ – by grace you have been saved" (Ephesians
2:4-5). Likewise, in the case of Paul's letter to Titus:

> But when the goodness and loving kindness of God our
> savior appeared, he saved us, not because of works done
> by us in righteousness, but according to his own mercy,
> by the washing of regeneration and renewal of the Holy
> Spirit, whom he poured out on us richly through Jesus
> Christ our Savior, so that being justified by his grace we
> might become heirs according to the hope of eternal life
> (Titus 3:4-7).

Jesus Christ redeems his people from slavery to sin and Satan,
beckoning and empowering them to follow and obey his perfect and
loving commands (see 1 John 5:3). With the gentle yoke of Christ

replacing the oppressive yoke of slavery to vile passions, we can declare with the psalmist:

> Oh give thanks to the Lord, for he is good, for his steadfast love endures forever! Let the redeemed of the Lord say so, whom he has redeemed from trouble and gathered in from the lands, from the east and from the west, from the north and from the south. . . . Let them thank the Lord for his steadfast love, for his wondrous works to the children of man! (Psalm 107:1-3, 8).

†

CHAPTER TWENTY-SIX

Christis the Only Way (Exclusivity)

In an age of pluralism, relativism, and postmodernism, the following declaration of Jesus Christ stabs into the eardrums of God-hating humanity: "I am the way, and the truth, and the life. No one comes to the Father except through me" (John 14:6). Though many may applaud the sacrificial love of Christ, the same will often hiss at the idea that Christ claims exclusive rights to truth. The idea that all paths lead to God is obliterated as a viable option for the Christian. Moreover, if Jesus Christ is who the Scriptures attest that he is (the exalted Son of God), then that option is void for all of humanity. Simple logic tells us that multiple claims to exclusive truth cannot all be correct. Either one is genuinely right and the others wrong, or they are all wrong. In light of Christ's claim to be the *only* way to the Father, the thought of placing him on lesser footing with other religious figures is struck down indefinitely. The Scriptures audaciously declare that "there is no other name under heaven given among men by which we must be saved" (Acts 4:12). Those who would denounce the testimony of Christ concerning himself as narrow-minded are answered in kind by Christ himself: "Enter by the narrow gate. For the gate is wide and the way is easy that leads to destruction, and those who enter by it are many" (Matthew 7:13). Jesus repeatedly and unashamedly made statements concerning his exclusive rights as the sole mediator between man and God. Writing about Christ's seemingly brazen comments, Piper states:

> The glory of Jesus Christ is that he is always out of sync with the world and therefore always relevant for the world. If he fit nicely, he would be of little use. The effort to remake the Jesus of the Bible so that he fits the spirit of one generation makes him feeble in another. Better to let him be what he is, because it is often the offensive side of Jesus that we need most. Especially offensive to the modern, western sentiment is the tough, blunt, fierce form of Jesus' love. People with thin skin would often have felt hurt by Jesus' piercing tongue. People who identify love only with soft and tender words and ways would have been repeatedly outraged by the singing, almost violent, language of the Lord.[66]

Let us pause for a moment and consider the implications of Christ's claims. If he is the prophesied Messiah who alone was able to satisfy the righteous wrath of God against sinners, then what would be more loving than for him to speak in clear, vivid terms regarding his identity? Praise be to his name, for he "was made manifest in the last times for the sake of you who through him are believers in God, who raised him from the dead and gave him glory, so that your faith and hope are in God" (1 Peter 1:20-21).

Christ's claims to be the sole possessor of access to God are, in a word, *scandalous*. It is the antithesis of cultural relevance to declare that all other truth claims are false. For this reason, the Bible states that Christ is "a stumbling block to the Jews and folly to the Gentiles" (1 Corinthians 1:23). Knowing that his sheep would be maligned at

---

66 Piper, *Seeing and Savoring Jesus Christ*, p. 93.

the utterance of such exclusive truth, Christ consoles them by saying, "Blessed are you when others revile you and persecute you and utter all kinds of evil against you falsely on my account" (Matthew 5:11). Regarding the offensive exclusivity of the gospel of Jesus Christ, Washer states:

> The true gospel is radically exclusive. Jesus is not *a* way; He is *the* way, and all other ways are no way at all. If Christianity would only move one small step toward a more tolerant ecumenicalism and exchange the definite article *the* for the indefinite article *a*, the scandal would be over, and the world and Christianity could become friends. However, whenever this occurs, Christianity ceases to be Christianity, Christ is denied, and the world is without a Savior.[67]

Jesus, by his life, death, resurrection, and ascension, is alone qualified to declare: "All things have been handed over to me by my Father, and no one knows the Son except the Father, and no one knows the Father except the Son and anyone to whom the Son chooses to reveal him" (Matthew 11:27).

---

67   Washer, *The Gospel's Power and Message*, p. 51.

✝

❦ PART FOUR ❧

MAN'S PROPER RESPONSE – THE APPLICATION OF REDEMPTION

"Now after John was arrested, Jesus came into Galilee, proclaiming the gospel of God, and saying, 'The time is fulfilled, and the kingdom of God is at hand; repent and believe in the gospel'" (Mark 1:15).

"You yourselves know how I lived among you the whole time from the first day that I set foot in Asia, serving the Lord with all humility and with tears and with trials that happened to me through the plots of the Jews; how I did not shrink from declaring to you anything that was profitable, and teaching you in public and from house to house, testifying both to Jews and to Greeks of repentance toward God and of faith in our Lord Jesus Christ" (Acts 20:18-21).

CHAPTER TWENTY-SEVEN

Turning From Sin, Trusting in Christ (Repentance and Faith)

As the weight of the previous chapters' contents are weighing on our minds and hearts, we can hear the voice of Jesus saying, "The time is fulfilled, and the kingdom of God is at hand; repent and believe the gospel" (Mark 1:15). The good news (gospel) that sinners can be declared righteous in God's sight through the sacrifice of the Lamb of God (Jesus) *demands* a response. This message, with its atomic power, will break or harden its hearers. Jesus does not leave room for apathetic responses to his claims. We must either believe or reject his claims to be the only one worthy and capable of declaring, "Son, your sins are forgiven" (Mark 2:5). Anyone who claims to have a fondness for Jesus yet does not joyfully embrace his claims about himself is not only offensive to God (John 3:36), but is also irrational. What then does it mean to *repent* and *believe?*

In Paul's first letter the church in Thessalonica, we see a wonderful depiction of repentance and faith in action: "For they themselves report concerning us the kind of reception we had among you, and how you turned to God from idols to serve the living and true God" (1 Thessalonians 1:9).

In this context, we observe two actions working in tandem to achieve the desired effect: the conversion of a sinner. Grudem states, "Conversion is our willing response to the gospel call, in which we sincerely repent of sins and place our trust in Christ for salvation."[68] The apostolic preaching of the gospel unabashedly included a call to repentance. Peter boldly proclaimed, "Repent therefore, and turn again, that your sins may be blotted out" (Acts 3:19). In like manner, Paul summarized the totality of his ministry by saying that he preached "to the Gentiles, that they should repent and turn to God, performing deeds in keeping with their repentance" (Acts 26:20). Repentance, at its core, involves "heartfelt sorrow for sin, a renouncing of it, and a sincere commitment to forsake it and walk in obedience to Christ."[69] This definition makes perfect sense in light of the previously cited passages.

The fruit of repentance (a changed life) that Paul called for is the outworking of the gift of repentance that is granted to the penitent sinner by a sovereign God (see 2 Timothy 2:25), otherwise repentance would be a meritorious act that earns us favor with God. Despite the tension between God calling "all people everywhere to repent" (Acts 17:30) and his gracious internal working via the Holy Spirit as the spiritually dead sinner hears the gospel (Romans 10:17, Ephesians 2:4-5), we acknowledge that Scripture calls for repentance as a necessary component of man's saving response to the gospel. Though some may object, saying that repentance is not required but merely an affirmation of the facts regarding Christ's life, death, and resurrection is necessary for salvation, Gilbert states it plainly and accurately:

> Repentance is not just an optional plug-in to the Christian life. It is absolutely crucial to it, marking out those who have been saved by God from those who have not. I have known many people who would say something like, "Yes,

---

68   Grudem, *Systematic Theology*, p. 709.

69   Ibid., p. 713.

I've accepted Jesus as Savior, so I'm a Christian. But I'm just not ready to accept him as Lord yet. I have some things to work through." In others words, they claimed that they could have faith in Jesus and be saved, and yet not repent of sin. If we understand repentance rightly, we'll see that the idea that you can accept Jesus as Savior but not Lord is nonsense. . . . To put one's faith in King Jesus is to renounce His enemies.[70]

Furthermore, repentance is not merely remorse; it is a heartfelt awareness that our sins are an offense to a holy God: "Against you, you only, have I sinned and done what is evil in your sight, so that you may be justified in your words and blameless in your judgments" (Psalm 51:4). Hearing the gospel and being awakened to the glorious, irresistible beauty of Christ produces "a repentance that leads to salvation without regret, whereas worldly grief produces death" (2 Corinthians 7:10). It was in the closing remarks of his most notable and enduring sermon that the iconic theologian Jonathan Edwards saw such godly sorrow and therefore called upon his congregation to turn from their sin: "Now, I cry to everyone who is outside of Christ, awake and flee from the wrath to come."[71]

It is at this juncture that we must ask, "Is forsaking my sin sufficient?" Others may interpose their own observation that certain passages of Scripture seem to intimate that faith is the only required response. The witness of Scripture illustrates that the authors held genuine repentance and faith to be inseparably linked. Jesus himself, just prior to his ascension into heaven, declared, "Thus it is written, that the Christ should suffer and on the third day rise from the dead, and that repentance and forgiveness of sins should be proclaimed in his name to all nations, beginning from

---

70 Gilbert, *What is the Gospel?* p. 79-80.

71 Jonathan Edwards, *Sinners in the Hands of an Angry God* (Alachua, FL: Bridge-Logos Publishers, 2003), p. 56.

Jerusalem" (Luke 24:46-47). In this passage, we see that forgiveness is proclaimed in the name of Christ and that those who would repent of their sins are called to trust in Jesus. This is the heartbeat of saving faith: "Saving faith is trust in Jesus Christ as a living person for forgiveness of sins and for eternal life with God."[72] Noting that the world often holds a fatally flawed viewed of faith, Gilbert satirically notes:

> Mystics believe in the power of stones and crystals. Crazy people believe in fairies. And Christians, well, they believe in Jesus. Read the Bible, though, and you'll find that faith is nothing like that caricature. Faith is not believing in something you can't prove, as so many people define it. It is, biblically speaking, *reliance*. A rock-solid, truth-grounded, promise-founded *trust* in the risen Jesus to save you from sin.[73]

The risen Christ, through the preaching of the gospel, beckons all men to repent of their sin and put their trust squarely upon him. Paul makes this clear in a passage that deals exclusively with the proclamation of the work of Christ on behalf of sinners: "How then will they call on him in whom they have not believed? And how are they to believe in him of whom they have never heard? And how are they to hear without someone preaching?" (Romans 10:14). Commenting on the role of the risen Christ, in light of Romans 10:14, Edmund P. Clowney attests that "Whom they have not heard is the right translation. . . . In preaching the gospel, Christ himself speaks to those who hear."[74] The gospel calls upon sin-enslaved rebels against a holy God to turn from their old master and serve a good, perfect, and ultimately alluring master, Jesus

---

72 Grudem, *Systematic Theology*, p. 710.

73 Gilbert, *What is the Gospel?* p. 74.

74 Edmund P. Clowney, *Preaching Christ in All of Scripture* (Wheaton, IL: Crossway, 2003), p. 46.

Christ. Regarding himself, Jesus declared that "whoever believes in him should not perish but have eternal life" (John 3:16). Inherent to this well-known verse of Scripture is the idea of trusting in the Person of Christ. Regarding Christ's call to believe "in him," Grudem notes that the "Greek phrase [πιστεύει σ ʿ αυτόν] could also be translated 'believe into him' with the sense of trust or confidence that goes *into* and rests *in* Jesus as a person."[75]

The gospel demands a response. Unfavorable sinners receive favor when they turn from their judgment-deserving sins and trust Jesus Christ as he is presented in Scripture and faithful gospel proclamation. When the Holy Spirit opens the crusted eyes of a sinner who has walked in daily darkness and he sees the horrid, gut-wrenching filth of sin upon him, he is broken by God's lawful indictment against him (Romans 7:11). In addition, the Spirit enables the sinner to see Christ in his full-orbed glory and empowers him to fall upon Christ in saving faith (John 6:44, Acts 16:14). Though it precedes repentance and faith, the miraculous rebirth of a sinner will be examined in the next chapter.

---

75 Grudem, *Systematic Theology*, p. 711.

CHAPTER TWENTY-EIGHT

The New Birth (Regeneration)

Though all men are commanded to repent and place their faith in the Person of Jesus Christ, the gloriously miraculous truth is that they, as *dead* sinners, are only able to do so after being raised from spiritual decay. Not unlike Lazarus, every son of Adam, being "dead in the trespasses and sins" (Ephesians 2:1) of his earthly pilgrimage, lies bound and foul in the grave cloths of iniquity. As the gospel is heralded, the risen and ascended Christ commands the corpse to "come out" (John 11:43). And so he does. The previous chapter (repentance and faith) expounded upon the necessary outworking of the topic at hand: *regeneration*. Here we will turn our attention to the miracle of the new birth that Jesus himself declared was part and parcel to genuine salvation: "Truly, truly, I say to you, unless one is born again he cannot see the kingdom of God" (John 3:3). In order to define our terms, we must incline our ear to the graveled voice of one of Christianity's giants, J. C. Ryle:

> Regeneration means, that change of heart and nature which a man goes through when he becomes a true Christian. I think there can be no question that there is an immense difference among those who profess and

call themselves Christians. Beyond all dispute there are always two classes in the outward Church – the class of those who are Christians in name and form only, and the class of those who are Christians in deed and in truth. All were not Israel who were called Israel, and all are not Christians who are called Christians.[76]

You would do well to note that Bishop Ryle wastes no time in addressing not only the act but the *nature* of regeneration. When God, by a secret act of his sovereign will, breathes life (repentance and faith) into a dead sinner through the preaching of the gospel (Romans 10:17) or the reading of the Scriptures (2 Timothy 3:15), they are qualitatively different. Paul states it plainly: "Therefore, if anyone is in Christ, he is a new creation. The old has passed away; behold, the new has come" (2 Corinthians 5:17).

The gift of the new birth is a sovereign act of grace on the part of God Almighty. We are no more able to raise ourselves from spiritual death than Lazarus was able to declare victory over his own demise. This is why Jesus expounds upon the mystery of the new birth in terms of sovereign causation: "The wind blows where it wishes, and you hear its sound, but you do not know where it comes from or where it goes. So it is with everyone who is born of the Spirit" (John 3:8). In this passage, Jesus is also pointing to the *effect* of the new birth. Someone may ask, "Why do Christians receive the new birth at various and diverse times?" To this inquiry, Ryle states:

> This change is not always given to believers at the same time in their lives. Some are born again when they are infants, and seem, like Jeremiah and John the Baptist, filled with the Holy Ghost even from their mother's

---

76 J. C. Ryle, *Regeneration: Being Born Again – What it Means and Why It's Necessary* (Scotland, UK: Christian Focus Publications, 2003), p. 11.

womb. Some few are born again in old age. The great majority of true Christians probably are born again after they grow up. A vast multitude of persons, it is to be feared, go down to the grave without having been born again at all. This change of heart does not always begin in the same way in those who go through it after they have grown up. With some, like the Apostle Paul, and the jailer at Philippi, it is a sudden and violent change, attended with much distress of mind. With others, like Lydia of Thyatira, it is more gentle and gradual: their winter becomes spring almost without their knowing how. With some the change is brought about by the Spirit working through afflictions or providential visitations. With others, and probably the greater number of true Christians, the word of God preached, or written, is the means of effecting it.[77]

In light of the *miraculous* nature of regeneration, the fact that vile sinners have received such marvelous grace should cause them to cease looking to the salvation of their sibling, neighbor, or parents in vain comparison and give glory to God for their own gracious calling, even if they are "untimely born" (1 Corinthians 15:8).

The regeneration of the sinner is as necessary as it is miraculous. To the praise of his glorious grace, the sovereign judge of all the earth chooses to raise to spiritual life his creatures who have willingly undone themselves and deserve only punishment (Romans 3:23). James exults in this truth: "Of his own will he brought us forth by the word of truth, that we should be a kind of firstfruits of his creatures" (James 1:18). The beauty of regeneration is this: though it is a sovereign act of God, we respond *willingly*. Prior to receiving saving grace, every sinner is blinded to God's glory: "In their case the god of this world has blinded the minds

---

77 Ibid., pp. 14-15.

of the unbelievers, to keep them from seeing the light of the gospel of the glory of Christ, who is the image of God" (2 Corinthians 4:4). Being dead in sin, they cannot see the irresistible glory of God. However, "For freedom Christ has set us free . . ." (Galatians 5:1). When repentance and faith are wrought in the life of the sinner, his eyes, like those of Paul (Acts 9:18), are cleansed and opened to behold the beauty of Christ. When we are able to see Christ in his breathtaking glory as the Savior, Redeemer, Mediator, Lamb of God, risen King, and the roaring Lion of Judah, we are drawn to him as beggars to food. Only God the Holy Spirit could bring about such a change of heart and will. Waxing brilliantly eloquent in his insights on the matter at hand, Piper states:

> God speaks not just to the ear and the mind, but he speaks to the heart. His internal heart-call opens the eyes of the blind heart, and opens the ears of the deaf heart, and causes Christ to appear as the supremely valuable person that he really is. So the heart freely and eagerly embraces Christ as the Treasure that he is. That's what God does when he calls us through the gospel (see 1 Peter 2:9; 5:10). . . . He called us from darkness to light and from death to life through the gospel and gave us eyes to see and ears to hear. He made the light of the glory of God in the face of Christ shine in our hearts through the gospel. And we believed. We embraced Christ for the Treasure that he is.[78]

Dear reader, if after your eyes have drunk from the pages of this meager work and if God has broken your heart and opened your eyes to the beauty of Christ, run to him! Do not stammer and pause as you gaze into the mystery of regeneration. If there is a measure of hatred for

---

78 John Piper, *Finally Alive* (Scotland, UK: Christian Focus Publications, Ltd., 2009), pp. 84-85.

your sin and a love of Christ that was absent prior to your reading this text, then heed the words of the Lord: "Come to me, all who labor and are heavy laden, and I will give you rest" (Matthew 11:28). Though your steps Christ-ward may seem clumsy and hobbled, recall the days of your infancy in which you determinedly trudged about the house. You were beckoned away from your props and called to rush to the open arms of your mother or father. If you have truly been made "alive together with Christ" (Ephesians 2:5), nothing will thwart your plodding toward the irresistible Son of God.

✝

CHAPTER TWENTY-NINE

Our New Legal Standing (Justification)

Ayoung man sits cross-armed in the second to the last pew. He stares with disdain at the banners hanging from the ceiling that have various names of God in Hebrew emblazoned upon them. The choirs' new rendition of a song written by a man long dead fades into white noise as he watches those hideous banners swaying gently in the breeze stirred up by the overworked ceiling fans. He has repeated this ritual every Sunday since his youth, pining for the day he dashes off to college. There he will find freedom from mandatory church attendance (and those smug banners). As the pastor thanks the choir, he opens his haggard Bible to the book of Acts. After a prayer for divine assistance, which sounded more like pleading, he began to expound upon a particular verse in chapter four: "And there is salvation in no one else, for there is no other name under heaven given among men by which we must be saved" (Acts 4:12). The last syllable scarcely leapt from the preacher's lips and the boy's chest heaved with new life. His cheeks were flushed and his hands clutched one another as his thoughts centered upon one reality: the need for salvation. He gently whispered, "I *must* be saved." The young man was utterly overcome by scenes of his sinful enactments that coursed through his mind. He found himself praying the very words of David that he had learned in Sunday school class four years earlier: "Against you, you only, have I sinned and done what is evil in your sight . . ." (Psalm 51:4). The Christ he once ignored had become his portion and his joy.

This young man was a benefactor of sovereign grace. As the gospel was proclaimed, he was brought to new life and with a "new heart and a new spirit" (Ezekiel 36:26) he reached out to Christ in faith. As we pan away from this small church and ascend heavenward, we will hear the angels glorifying God with thunderous enthusiasm as he declares this once God-hating boy to be *not guilty* in his courtroom. In like manner, every sinner who repents and turns to Christ with genuine saving faith will be justified. Paul declares this truth in a singular verse that has come to be known as the *Golden Chain*: "And those whom he predestined he also called, and those whom he called he also *justified*, and those whom he justified he also glorified" (Romans 8:30, emphasis added). Justification is "an instantaneous legal act of God in which he (1) thinks of our sins as forgiven and Christ's righteousness as belonging to us, and (2) declares us to be righteous in his sight."[79] In his book, *Redemption Accomplished and Applied*, John Murray states:

> The meaning of the word "justify," therefore, in the epistle to the Romans, and therefore in the epistle which more than any other book in Scripture unfolds the doctrine, is to declare to be righteous. Its meaning is entirely removed from the thought of making upright or holy or good or righteous. This is what is meant when we insist that justification is forensic. The main point of such terms is to distinguish between the kind of action which justification involves and the kind of action involved in regeneration. Regeneration is an act of God in us; justification is an act of God with respect to us.

---

79 Grudem, *Systematic Theology*, p. 723.

The distinction is like that of the distinction between the act of a surgeon and the act of a judge. The surgeon, when he removes an inward cancer, does something in us. That is not what a judge does – he gives a verdict regarding our judicial status. If we are innocent he declares accordingly. The purity of the gospel is bound up with the recognition of this distinction. If justification is confused with regeneration or sanctification, then the door is opened for the perversion of the gospel at its centre. Justification is still the article of the standing or falling Church.[80]

Murray's point must not be missed or skewed: justification is an instantaneous act and is distinct from regeneration and sanctification (this term will be examined in a later chapter). When God justifies a sinner, he thinks of that sinner's sins as forgiven:

Therefore, since we have been justified by faith, we have peace with God through our Lord Jesus Christ. . . Since, therefore, we have now been justified by his blood, much more shall we be saved by him from the wrath of God. For if while we were enemies we were reconciled to God by the death of his Son, much more, now that we are reconciled, shall we be saved by his life (Romans 5:1, 9-10).

As if this fact were not sufficiently glorious, justification also bears the idea of *imputation*. In this, the perfect righteousness of Jesus Christ is reckoned or imputed to the sinner: "And to the one who does not work but believes in him who justifies the ungodly, his faith is counted as righteousness" (Romans 4:5). Standing before the throne of God's white-hot holiness donning the garments of the exalted Christ is the very image

---

80   John Murray, *Redemption Accomplished and Applied* (Grand Rapids, MI: Wm. B. Eerdmans Publishing Company, 1955), p. 121.

that fuels Paul's praise: "There is therefore now no condemnation for those who are in Christ Jesus" (Romans 8:1). We are not called to work toward justification as an end in itself; we are declared to be righteous the instant we are brought to new life through faith. It is with this illustrious truth in mind that we incline our ears to the voice of David: "Blessed is the one whose transgression is forgiven, whose sin is covered. Blessed is the man against whom the Lord counts no iniquity, and in whose spirit there is no deceit" (Psalm 32:1-2).

Chapter Thirty

Our New Familial Status (Adoption)

During the celebration of Passover, a traditional song that dates back more than a thousand years is sung by all in attendance. *Dayenu* roughly translates into English as *it would have been enough.* This upbeat song commemorates the wonderful works of redemption that God wrought on behalf of the Jewish people: freedom from slavery in Egypt, the giving of the Torah, etc. The song's aim is to convey the abundant goodness of the Lord toward his people in that even if he had only given them one gracious gift, it would have been enough. With this in mind, we now turn our attention to the Scriptures as they continue to spring forth fresh mercy and grace:

> For you did not receive the spirit of slavery to fall back into fear, but you have received the Spirit of adoption as sons, by whom we cry, "Abba! Father!" The Spirit himself bears witness with our spirit that we are the children of God, and if children, then heirs – heirs of God and fellow heirs with Christ, provided we suffer with him in order that we may also be glorified with him (Romans 8:15-17).

After systematically building a case against fallen humanity in the first three chapters of *Romans*, Paul methodically expounds upon justification by faith (chapter four), the product of justification (chapter five), the exchange of masters (chapter six), and the battle against the flesh (chapter seven). Having laid a firm, theologically sound foundation upon which to build, Paul exults in the reality of being adopted by God the Father. If Christ had simply made atonement for our sins and given us his righteousness in order that we might all be doormen in the Lord's palace, it would have been sufficient – *Dayenu*! As it is, we have been brought near to the bosom of God and blessed with a name that even angels long to hear: *beloved*. Elsewhere in his epistles to the churches, Paul highlights the believer's status as a child of God by merit of his adoption:

> I mean that the heir, as long as he is a child, is no different from a slave, though he is the owner of everything, but he is under guardians and managers until the date set by his father. In the same way we also, when we were children, were enslaved to the elementary principles of the world. But when the fullness of time had come, God sent forth his Son, born of a woman, born under the law, to redeem those who were under the law, so that we might receive adoption as sons. And because you are sons, God has sent the Spirit of his Son into our hearts, crying, "Abba! Father!" So you are no longer a slave, but a son, and if a son, then an heir through God (Galatians 4:1-7).

Not only is the adoption of his children part of the plan of redemption, it was set in motion in the mind of God in the annals of eternity: "He predestined us for adoption as sons through Jesus Christ, according to the purpose of his will" (Ephesians 1:5). With the chime of the hammer that drove the nails into the hands and feet of Christ ringing in our ears, we can do no more than to utter *Dayenu*. The severity of the punishment that our sin excited, the view of Christ shedding his perfect blood on behalf of God-hating rebels, and the declaration of "Justified!" that echoes in the courtroom of God's chamber would have been sufficient. Nevertheless, the Scriptures bear witness to the stunning fact that God not only predestined the redemption of his people, but their adoption as well.

The adoption of justified sinners is yet another shining gem in the crown of the gospel. How utterly powerful and magnificently sufficient is the blood of Christ! One drop is able to atone for a universe of sinners because of the inherent quality of the sinless lifeblood of the God-man. It is also sufficiently powerful to appease the righteous indignation of a holy God insofar that he not only dips his royal scepter in the direction of his subjects, but beckons them to enter his courts as sons and daughters! When we, as recipients of adoptive grace, scan the throne room of our Father, we see other grateful souls donning gowns of righteousness not unlike our own:

> And they sang a new song, saying, "Worthy are you to take the scroll and open its seals, for you were slain, and by your blood you ransomed people for God from every tribe and language and people and nation, and you have made them a kingdom and priests to our God, and they shall reign on the earth" (Revelation 5:9).

We are adopted as individuals and yet are ushered into the *family* of God. Men, women, and children from every tribe, nation, and tongue will be represented before the throne of God. The reality of adoption, therefore, should inform every true believer's disposition toward other Christians. Writing on this very topic, Milton Vincent notes:

> The more I experience the gospel, the more there develops within me a yearning affection for my fellow-Christians who are also participating in the glories of the gospel. . . . Indeed, I love my fellow-Christians not simply because

of the gospel, but I love them best when I am loving them with the gospel! And I do this not merely by speaking gospel words to them, but also by living before them and generously relating to them in a gospel manner. Imparting my life to them in this way, I thereby contribute to their experience of the power, the Spirit, and the full assurance of the gospel. By preaching the gospel to myself each day, I nurture the bond that unites me with the my brothers and sisters for whom Christ died, and I also keep myself well-versed in the raw materials with which I may actively love them in Christ.[81]

The saving of sinners would have been sufficient. The adoption of justified sinners is *astounding*.

---

81   Milton Vincent, *A Gospel Primer for Christians: Learning to See the Glories of God's Love* (Bemidji, MN: Focus Publishing, 2008), pp. 22-23.

CHAPTER THIRTY-ONE

Growth in Godliness (Sanctification)

When the Lord, through the Holy Spirit, births a soul anew, does he content himself to set the spiritual infant aside and wait for it to grow unaided? No, he does not. The Scriptures testify that "he who began a good work in you will bring it to completion at the Day of Jesus Christ" (Philippians 1:6). The process whereby the Holy Spirit (as the primary cause) and man (as the secondary cause) become progressively free from sin and conformed to the image of Jesus Christ is called *sanctification*. The word itself denotes an activity that was completed in the past, but has ongoing effects. Therefore, Scripture speaks in various ways regarding the believer's sanctification. In some instances, our sanctification is portrayed as a completed event: "And such were some of you. But you were washed, *you were sanctified*, you were justified in the name of the Lord Jesus Christ and by the Spirit of our God" (1 Corinthians 6:11, emphasis added). Elsewhere the Scriptures depict our sanctification as a current reality: ". . . For just as you once presented your members as slaves to impurity and to lawlessness, so now present your members as slaves to righteousness leading to sanctification" (Romans 6:19). Scripturally speaking, believers were sanctified and are being sanctified.

The process of sanctification will not be completed in this life. Though believers are commanded to "work out your own salvation with fear and trembling" (Philippians 2:12), they will continue to battle against sin throughout their earthly journey. Writing to believers throughout Asia Minor, the apostle John plainly states: "If we say we have no sin, we deceive ourselves, and the truth is not in us" (1 John 1:8). The life of a genuine Christian is one of both contented joy and spiritual warfare. Paul, on two specific accounts, calls the churches to not only identify their sin, but to murder it. To the Romans he writes, "For if you live according to the flesh you will die, but if by the Spirit you put to death the deeds of the body, you will live" (Romans 8:13). Similarly, Paul instructs the Colossian Christians by stating, "Put to death therefore what is earthly in you: sexual immorality, impurity, passion, evil desire, and covetousness, which is idolatry" (Colossians 3:5). Offering his penetrating insight on Paul's exhortations to the churches, John Owen writes:

> The intention of the apostle in this prescription of the duty mentioned, is, that the mortification of indwelling sin, remaining in our mortal bodies, in order that it may not have life and power to bring forth the works or deeds of the flesh, is the constant duty of believers.[82]

Owen rightly identifies the call to mortify (kill) our sinful desires as the duty of every genuine believer. As one reads through the New Testament, it becomes glaringly clear that the Lord graciously and repetitively calls his children to actively pursue Christ-likeness. The writer of Hebrews, for example, encourages Christians to this end by way of analogy:

---

82 John Owen, *The Mortification of Sin* (Scotland, UK: Christian Focus Publications Ltd., 2010), p. 23.

Therefore, since we are surrounded by so great a cloud of witnesses, let us also lay aside every weight, and sin which clings so closely, and let us run with endurance the race that is set before us. . . . Strive for peace with everyone, and for the holiness without which no one will see the Lord (Hebrews 12:1, 14).

Peter also instructs believers regarding their daily conduct: "But as he who called you is holy, you also be holy in all your conduct, since it is written, 'You shall be holy, for I am holy'" (1 Peter 1:15-16). The totality of Scripture indicates that the expectation of the apostles for the genuine believers was that their sanctification will increase as they mature.

The seemingly paradoxical (though *antinomy* would be more fitting) truth of our sanctification lies in the fact that every individual follower of Christ is commanded to *actively* pursue holiness while being the *passive* recipient of God's sanctifying activity. Harkening back to Paul's letter to the Philippians, we see a clear portrayal of God's internal work of sanctification in the lives of his children: "For it is God who works in you, both to will and to work for his good pleasure" (Philippians 2:13). Of the Thessalonian Christians, Paul states, "But we ought always to give thanks to God for you, brothers beloved by the Lord, because God chose you as the firstfruits to be saved, through *sanctification by the Spirit* and belief in the truth" (2 Thessalonians 2:13, emphasis added). Of the dispersed and persecuted believers of Peter's day he writes, "According to the foreknowledge of God the Father, in the *sanctification of the Spirit*, for obedience to Jesus Christ and for sprinkling with his blood: May grace and peace be multiplied to you" (1 Peter 1:2, emphasis added). The Scriptures testify that God is not only able to save a man, he is able to conform that same man to the image of his beloved Son throughout the course of his life. Of the Holy Spirit's role in the sanctification of believers, Jerry Bridges notes:

The transformation process the Bible describes is much more than a change of conduct or improved human morality; it is actually a work of the Holy Spirit in the very core of our being. In the only two instances in Scripture where the word *transformed* is used, it occurs both times in the passive voice. We are *being* transformed (see 2 Corinthians 3:18), and we are to *be* transformed (see Romans 12:2). In both instances, we are the object, not the agent, of the transformation process; the agent is the Holy Spirit.[83]

We are being shaped by the inner working of the Holy Spirit on a continual basis. At the same time, we are called to faithfully obey the commands of Scripture that instruct us to actively pursue holiness. It is in this mysterious yet axiomatic truth that we see ourselves "being transformed into the same image [of Christ] from one degree of glory to another. For this comes from the Lord who is the Spirit" (2 Corinthians 3:18).

---

83 Bridges, *The Transforming Power of the Gospel*, p. 89.

✝

✑ PART FIVE ✑

THAT YOU MAY KNOW –
ASSURANCE OF SALVATION

"Examine yourselves, to see whether you are in the faith. Test yourselves. Or do you not realize this about yourselves, that Jesus Christ is in you? – unless indeed you fail to meet the test!" (2 Corinthians 13:5).

"I write these things to you who believe in the name of the Son of God that you may know that you have eternal life" (1 John 5:13).

✝

CHAPTER THIRTY-TWO

The Mirror of God's Word (Defining Biblical Assurance)

By a slow process of theological erosion, the waters of secularism and liberal theology have defaced the landscape of the church's doctrinal understanding of truth once held in high esteem. One of the largest and most detrimental of the casualties is the marginalization (or complete abandonment) of teaching on the assurance of salvation. After reading and musing about the truth presented in the previous chapters, one may begin to ask the obvious question: "How do I *know* that I have repented and believed the gospel?" For many professing Christians, their assurance of salvation rests in a date written on the inside of their Bible that serves as a landmark pointing to a time when they were sincere in their faith. Others reference their baptism (infant or adult), church membership, or their family's spiritual pedigree in order to gain some sense of assurance regarding their relationship with God. Still others look to more subtle and insidiously misleading offers of assurance such as serving in church leadership, staying busy with church-related projects, or even their private devotional life. Though many of these engagements are not inherently bad, wrong, or damaging, they are damnable substitutes for true, saving faith. So at this juncture, the question remains regarding what biblical assurance *is* and how one is to *obtain* it.

Biblical assurance refers to true believers having an internal sense, based upon specific evidences in their lives, that they are *truly* born-again and will persevere in trusting Christ alone for salvation throughout their lives.[84] This internal sense that is spoken of is to be understood as one that aligns with scriptural truth. Though believers may sense or feel many things, they are called to "test everything; hold fast to what is good" (1 Thessalonians 5:21). This is a crucial point to make in light of Scripture's description of the unregenerate heart: "The heart is deceitful above all things, and desperately sick; who can understand it?" (Jeremiah 17:9). It should likewise be noted that the evidences referenced are the observable products of an *internal* change: "But the fruit of the Spirit is love, joy, peace, patience, kindness, goodness, faithfulness, gentleness, self-control; against such things there is no law" (Galatians 5:22-23). Being versed in the Scripture's testimony regarding the fruit of genuine salvation will enable the sincere evangelist to comfort the afflicted and afflict the comfortable.

Strong language is necessary to convey the seriousness of this topic. The soul is the most precious organism that we are called to handle and we must treat each one as if it were made of porcelain. Jesus, the master evangelist, would encourage his disciples with gentle words of affirmation: "All that the Father gives me will come to me, and whoever comes to me I will never cast out" (John 6:37). Jesus would also not hesitate to speak in no uncertain terms regarding the fruit of conversion: "Not everyone who says to me, 'Lord, Lord,' will enter the kingdom of heaven, but the one who does the will of my Father who is in heaven'" (Matthew 7:21). It is here that we must return to our definition of biblical assurance. Everyone who professes to have

---

84 Grudem, *Systematic Theology*, p. 1236.

repented of their sin and placed their faith in the person and work of Jesus Christ for their salvation should increasingly sense that the very faith they profess is progressively changing them internally.

Regarding the obtaining of assurance, we must note that the pursuit of assurance is a positive endeavor. Though assurance is often presented with a negative tone (as a warning), it is equally a means of great joy for the believer. Writing about the pursuit of biblical assurance, J. C. Ryle notes:

> Assurance . . . is not a mere fancy of feeling. It is not the result of high animal spirits, or a sanguine temperament of body. It is a positive gift of the Holy Ghost, bestowed without reference to men's bodily frames or constitutions, and a gift which every believer in Christ ought to aim at and seek after. The Word of God appears to me to teach that a believer may arrive at an assured confidence with regard to his own salvation. I would lay it down fully and broadly, that a true Christian, a converted man, may reach that comfortable degree of faith in Christ, that in general he shall feel entirely confident as to the pardon and safety of his soul, shall seldom be troubled with doubts, seldom be distracted with hesitation, seldom be distressed by anxious questionings, and, in short, though vexed by many an inward conflict with sin, shall look forward to death without trembling, and to judgment without dismay.[85]

What a blessed reality! What child of God would not want to possess such peace of mind and heart? The thought of a genuine, blood-bought child of God lacking true assurance of his most hard-wrought salvation is as offensive as a false convert taking to their breast a viperous sense

---

85 J. C. Ryle, *Assurance: How to Know You are a Christian* (Scotland, UK: Christian Focus Publications, 1989), pp. 17-18.

of assurance that is vain. Perhaps this very fact motivated Peter's words when he exhorted believers to "be all the more diligent to make your calling and election sure" (2 Peter 1:10).

The apostles were humble men and yet possessed an abiding sense of confident assurance. Paul unhesitatingly addressed the Corinthian believers regarding his potential demise:

> For we *know* that if the tent that is our earthly home is destroyed, we have a building from God, a house not made with hands, eternal in the heavens. . . . We *know* that while we are at home in the body we are away from the Lord (2 Corinthians 5:1, 6, emphasis added).

The apostle speaks in a similar tone when addressing young Timothy: ". . . But I am not ashamed, for I *know* whom I have believed, and I am *convinced* that he is able to guard until that Day what has been entrusted to me" (2 Timothy 1:12, emphasis added). It is in this verse that we observe the core of assurance: a present and abiding trust in Jesus Christ alone for salvation. It is not enough to hearken back to a spiritual experience of years past and claim that you believed then if you do not believe now. This abiding trust in the Lord Jesus produces the external fruit that was mentioned previously: "I am the vine; you are the branches. Whoever abides in me and I in him, he it is that bears much fruit, for apart from me you can do nothing" (John 15:5).

The assurance of salvation, being an internal sense that one has been born-again, is a gracious gift to God's people to encourage them as they persevere unto Christian maturity: ". . . for if you practice these qualities you will never fall" (2 Peter 1:10). It is to be sought after as a means of grace that leads to joyful perseverance. It is also a doctrine that should be impressed upon the professing Christian in order to bring about healthy (and potentially saving) scriptural self-examination. In the concluding chapter of this book, we will examine a portion of Scripture that offers comforting, yet challenging insight regarding true biblical assurance.

CHAPTER THIRTY-THREE

Taking the Test (Lessons from First John)

John, as the last surviving apostle and well-aged in years, displays the compassionate heart of a father as he writes his epistle to the congregations of Asia Minor. The churches were, at the time of John's writing, being infiltrated by an early form of Gnosticism that maintained that Christ was not fully human. This was due to their belief that the physical realm (i.e., Christ's body) was inherently evil and the spiritual realm was inherently good. The apostle John, in order to ward off the infection of such heresy, writes a letter to the churches that is loving, strikingly clear, and useful for both gaining genuine assurance of conversion as well as identifying false converts.

The book of *First John* contains a number of seemingly *quid pro quo* (this for that) statements that, when taken together, form a series of tests that enable the sincere inquirer to obtain a joyful sense of assurance. These same tests can also tip over the idols of false hope that deluded persons have set up in their hearts. In either case, it is the sovereign grace of God to bestow contented peace upon his children as well as to work repentance into the heart of an awakened sinner. Regarding the pursuit of biblical assurance in the examination of texts such as the one at hand, J. C. Ryle writes:

> Reader, what shall we say to these things? I desire to speak with all humility on any controverted point. I feel that I am only a poor fallible child of Adam myself. But I must say, that in the passages I have just quoted I see something far higher than the mere "hopes" and "trusts" with which so many believers appear content in this day. I see the language of persuasion, confidence, knowledge, nay, I may almost say, of certainty. And I feel, for my own part, if I may take these Scriptures in their plain, obvious meaning, the doctrine of assurance is true. But my answer, furthermore, to all who dislike the doctrine of assurance, as bordering on presumption, is this: it can hardly be presumption to tread in the steps of Peter and Paul, of Job and John. They were all imminently humble and lowly-minded men, if ever any were; and yet they all speak of their own state with an assured hope.[86]

One of the first tests that John presents to his audience appears in the second chapter: "And by this we know that we have come to know him, if we keep his commandments. Whoever says, 'I know him' but does not keep his commandments is a liar, and the truth is not in him" (1 John 2:3-4). We would do well to note that John again uses the word "know" as opposed to hope, or think, or assume, etc. Clearly, assurance is something that is tangible and qualitative. Following the leading of the Holy Spirit as a means of gaining assurance is echoed by Peter: "As obedient children, do not be conformed to the passions of your former ignorance, but as he who called you is holy, you also be holy in all your conduct" (1 Peter 1:14-15). Habitual, *though imperfect*, obedience to God's

---

86 Ibid., pp. 26-27.

Word should mark the life of every true Christian. Lest we deem this to be mere laborious religion, John elsewhere clarifies the nature of our obedience: "For this is the love of God, that we keep his commandments. And his commandments are not burdensome" (1 John 5:3). A desire to obey the Lord is the joyful fruit of a changed heart. The exhortations of Scripture that we once saw as foolishness and cruel self-restriction (see Ephesians 2:1-3) become a means of welcome guidance from a loving savior: "Come to me, all who labor and are heavy laden, and I will give you rest" (Matthew 11:28).

Secondly, the book of *First John* states that a true Christian will not (cannot) habitually sin. Before pressing forward, we must look back to John's earlier statement in order to establish an often misunderstood truth: "If we say we have no sin, we deceive ourselves, and the truth is not in us" (1 John 1:8). Clearly the apostle does not envision the life of a true Christian as one of sinless perfection. Having established this truth, let us turn our attention to John's third chapter where he expounds upon the qualitative outworking of regeneration in the life of a true Christian:

> Whoever makes a practice of sinning is of the devil, for the devil has been sinning from the beginning. The reason the Son of God appeared was to destroy the works of the devil. No one born of God makes a practice of sinning, for God's seed abides in him, and he cannot keep on sinning because he has been born of God. By this it is evident who are the children of God, and who are the children of the devil: whoever does not practice righteousness is not of God, nor is the one who does not love his brother (1 John 3:8-10).

Due to the gracious, powerful working of the Holy Spirit in sanctifying a true believer, he is no longer able to live at peace with his formerly treasured sins. Paul echoes this sentiment in his letter to the Roman Christians:

But thanks be to God, that you who were once slaves of
sin have become obedient from the heart to the standard
of teaching to which you were committed, and, having
been set free from sin, have become slaves of righteousness
(Romans 6:17-18).

Though every true believer will struggle with sin throughout his
earthly pilgrimage, the reality of the new birth (John 3:3) is such that he,
as a slave of righteousness, will be compelled to engage in warfare against
the "sin which clings so closely" (Hebrews 12:1).

Thirdly, the book of *First John* reveals a wonderful reality concerning
the reborn believer: a genuine love for others. John tells us that "We
know we have passed out of death into life, because we love the brothers.
Whoever does not love abides in death" (1 John 3:14). In this singular
verse a clear correlation is made between one's assurance of faith and his
love for others. Having tasted, relished, and embraced the grace of God
in their unmerited salvation, true Christians are marked by habitual
love. This correlation is clearly seen in John's fourth chapter: "In this
is love, not that we have loved God but that he loved us and sent his
Son to be the propitiation for our sins" (1 John 4:10). This passage also
denotes a special love for other Christians. Christ himself spoke of this
unique bond when he told his followers, "By this all people will know
that you are my disciples, if you have love for one another" (John 13:35).
Peter also points to this supernatural affection between Christians
as he exhorts the churches in dispersion: "Honor everyone. Love the
brotherhood. Fear God. Honor the emperor" (1 Peter 2:17). A heart
changed by the miraculous work of the Holy Spirit (see 2 Corinthians
5:17) is expected to be a heart that beats with fond affection for others,
saved and unsaved.

Lastly, the apostle John goes on to say that though the hearts of
true Christians are full of compassion, their affections will not be set
upon the things of this world: "Do not love the world or the things in

the world. If anyone loves the world, the love of the Father is not in him" (1 John 2:15). Commenting on this verse, Donald S. Whitney states:

> Unbelievers love the world and plunge into it because it's all they have. And the more they realize they won't be here forever, the more they immerse themselves into the world to find meaning, hope, pleasure, and satisfaction. They discover, of course, that the world can't fill the hole in their heart, but they keep trying because they don't have anything else (unless they come to Christ). . . . Christians, however, feel less at home in this world the more they grow spiritually. They also look increasingly toward their true and eternal home, the Celestial City.[87]

A similar warning is put forth by James: "You adulterous people! Do you not know that friendship with the world is enmity with God? Therefore whoever wishes to be a friend of the world makes himself an enemy of God" (James 4:4). What a blessing of contented assurance it is when a genuine believer sees his affections turning (in increasing measure) away from the passions of the world and toward the living God! A desire to obey the Lord's commands, sensitivity to sin, tender affection for others, and a growing disdain for worldly pleasures are, according to the apostle John, gracious means of obtaining the assurance that we have passed from death to life.

---

87 Donald S. Whitney, *How Can I Be Sure I'm a Christian?* (Colorado Springs, CO: NavPress, 1994), p. 56.

AFTERWORDS

It is my prayer that the Holy Spirit has worked in your heart and mind as you have read the pages of this humble book so that you see, love, embrace, and follow the Lord Jesus Christ. Though I may never know how or if the Lord used this book to glorify his name through the saving of sinners, it is nonetheless put forth with the eager expectation that he would do so. To my own children, if you are reading this, please know that I love you dearly and pray that the old truth presented in this work would be the "power of God for salvation" (Romans 1:16) for you as well as my grandchildren to come. Though I am not a prophet, I feel that I can safely assume that secularization, man-centered preaching, and a low view of Scripture will increasingly permeate the religious landscape of the future. Though God will undoubtedly fulfill his purposes for his people in spite of this coming apostasy (Philippians 1:6), I am honor bound to pass on the truth of the glorious gospel to all who come after me. Whether you are my biological child or a perfect stranger, I pray that you come to relish the bloody, offensive, foolish cross of Christ as the public declaration that God is "just and the justifier of the one who has faith in Jesus" (Romans 3:26).